My Mother's Luck

BY RON WADEY

ABOUT THE AUTHOR

Ron Wadey is a successful bookmaker with more than forty years' experience in the game. He started out working in betting shops at eighteen years of age, and then started to build his own empire of shops. He sold his last shop before the big betting-shop collapse, and moved onto the racetracks. He now has successful pitches at many of the country's most prestigious meetings. With a ready wit, and a rare ability to take losing gracefully, Ron is a much-loved and well-respected member of the racing community. He has three grown-up children. Now in his seventies, Ron still enjoys life to the full. He walks his dog, Dessie, several miles every day, and is still beating opponents on the tennis court with his prodigious backhand!

To Sarah & Alex

Best Wishes for

Christmas & New Year

from Ron Ron.

23.11.22

First published in Great Britain 2020

Copyright © Ron Wadey 2020

All rights reserved. No part of this publication may be reproduced,
stored in a retrieval system, or transmitted in any form or by any means, electronic,
mechanical, photocopying, recording or otherwise, without prior
permission in writing from the publisher

British Library Cataloguing in Publication Data

A CIP catalogue record for this book is available upon request
from the British Library

ISBN: 978-1-5272-7327-6

Ron Wadey has asserted his right under the Copyright,
Design and Patents Act 1988 to be identified as the author of this work

Cover design and typeset by Fusion Graphic Design Ltd

Paper from responsible sources

For my children, Colin, David and Michelle,
and my grandchildren, Ashley, Adam,
Daniel, Lauren, Jack and Polly.

FOR GEOFF CONNOR

I'd like to dedicate this book to an old friend, Geoff Connor. We only lived ten or twenty yards away when we were growing up, and were good friends through school. Geoff is just a few years older than me, but we stayed friends for many years. We lost touch – as you do – but then out of the blue, I heard about Geoff again...

Someone told me he'd had his leg amputated and was waiting for a prosthetic replacement. So I found out where he was living and went to see him. It must have been thirty years since we'd last met, and I wasn't sure what sort of man Geoff would be. Well, the experience he's been through told me exactly what sort of man he was – he was an inspiration. Geoff is as honest as the day is long, and despite everything that has happened to him, he wouldn't let anything get him down. Geoff is as modest as ever, and still has a great sense of humour.

I've met a lot of fantastic people in my life, but I think that Geoff exemplifies the kind of person we all aspire to be, and that's why I'm proud to dedicate this book to him.

IN MEMORY OF ALAN SMITH

I didn't have a brother, but I had a cousin – Alan Smith – on my dad's side of the family. He didn't have a brother either, but the two of us were like brothers. I used to go and stay at his mother's house in Kibworth, Leicestershire in the school holidays.

He was a little older than me and I was always keen to see how he did in life. I'm sure there was a little element of me wanting to keep up with him at first too. He started out with one taxi and got a few more, then he bought a coach. He went on to get some good contracts – first the Leicester Prison contract, then the Leicester City Football Club contract. So half the time he was transporting a load of football players about, and the rest of the time he was transporting the prisoners!

I used to drop in to see Alan on my way back from Newmarket, and he would come and see me for a drink and a chance to catch up. He certainly liked his whisky and one night at my previous house he drank a little too much, and he left a memento of that night on the floor!

In 2009, Alan was diagnosed with cancer. He was on chemotherapy tablets, and we all thought the cancer was under control, but then his daughter rang me broken-hearted, to say that he was in intensive care. He died three days later from swine flu.

Alan was a fine man, and I learned a lot about his attitude to life and his hard work ethic, and I'm proud to have had him as an unofficial brother.

CONTENTS

FOREWORD

By Frank James Seymour

I assisted Ron Wadey in launching a successful expansion period in what, as you're about to read, was an eventful business life. Our working relationship started in the early 1980s. We came to an arrangement for him to close his own betting office in Warrington in exchange for taking over one of my betting offices in Upholland, then operated by William Hill. I quickly formed my opinion of him and found Ron to be knowledgeable of the industry, and clearly a man on a mission. He certainly knew what he wanted and had a clear direction of where he was heading. I also considered him to be totally honest; he was a man that I instinctively knew I could trust and conduct business with. Later as I got to know him better – and my first impressions were confirmed – I also had to acknowledge that he was quite a raconteur. When Ron is in full flow it can sometimes be hard to get a word in edgeways. That together with a slightly wicked sense of humour makes him good company.

We were strangers when we met to thrash out that mutually beneficial contract but it was the start of a long-standing personal and professional association, and we have been friends ever since that day. We really got together again from around 1990, when I was acting as a consultant to the independent betting office sector. Ron was ready for expansion and sought my assistance to obtain a number of new licences to increase his representation. The result of this was five high-quality shops in his estate.

Ron's forte was his great understanding of what made a successful betting office that punters felt at home in. His talent and ability, built up over many years of experience, enabled him to operate those shops in an absolutely professional manner, from customer service to first-class shop marketing. He became a pioneer within the betting industry with his innovative creation of the 'BOG' concession (Best Odds Guaranteed). I believe the inspiration for BOG was that TV advertisement around at the time for double glazing: BOGOF (Buy one, get one free). In the early Eighties, the industry introduced betting on early morning prices where the customer could take a set price for his selection irrespective of what the starting price (SP) would be – SP being the standard form of settling bets. Ron's concession gave the customer the best of both prices, whichever was the greater – a fantastic marketing edge. It wasn't long before the large companies followed suit, but naming theirs GSP – Greater SP. He followed that by extending his marketing campaign, advertising his shops as 'Five shops under one roof'. He gave his customers the choice of any price offered by himself or the major companies together with the best odds guaranteed, if the SP was higher. He was questioned on this by a little old lady who enquired, "I know this is a betting office, but what are the other shops in here as well?"

Ron never undermined that trust I put in him at our very first meeting, and in 1996 I moved on from my consultancy business and became MD of a Wirral-based betting company, David Pluck. We stayed friends and he made a promise to me that if he was ever to sell on his business, he would give me an opportunity to make an offer for it. That opportunity arose when he decided to sell four of his five shops and move on to new ventures. He had received an acceptable offer from one of the PLCs and called me to inform me of the details. He gave me the opportunity to match their price on one proviso: that I would also have to take on – as part of the deal – a small bistro he had opened in Warrington. Didn't I mention earlier that he is also a crafty little devil? And as you will read, when we did the first deal in Warrington, he wanted a bit more than a straight swap and managed to squeeze an additional two grand out of me! Well, after all these years, I can now exclusively reveal that I actually had a budget of £5K to conclude that deal. I think that makes us 1–1, Ron!

Ron seemed to enjoy the early days of his semi-retirement and indulged his love of greyhound racing by becoming an owner. Any visitors to his home around this time would be royally entertained with stories of his beloved greyhounds and their successes and he enjoyed any opportunity to show off the display of trophies they had won.

You will read about Ron's sporting achievements, and he is still an active tennis player today, but his next serious venture came when he decided to become an on-course bookmaker. Like everything in his career, he went into this venture with the same enthusiasm and energy that he has displayed throughout his life. He quickly got to grips with the intricacies of on-course bookmaking which is a world away from the betting office scene. It is of no surprise to me that he is enjoying the same level of success in this venture as he did in his betting offices.

The betting industry has given us many characters over the years at all levels, but it is sad to say that many of them have long left the scene with not too many coming through to replace them. If you look back into the history of licensed betting offices, you will see that, at the inception of legalised betting shops in 1961, there were around 20,000 premises licences issued. The majority of those business were operated by independent bookmakers and were a breeding ground for so many great characters. Today there are some 8,500 betting offices, of which 13% are operated by independents against 87% operated by the large companies. Most of the large operators are now run by accountants and not the traditional bookmaker. When you read this book and enjoy Ron's recollections of some of the events in his life, you will see for yourself that he is indeed befitting of the tag of a 'character' in his own right. Or, as he himself – with his slightly wicked sense of humour – put it on his business card:

RON WADEY – BOOKMAKER. A LEGEND IN HIS OWN MIND.

I think that speaks volumes of the man! I can safely say that no man has worked harder for his achievements, and he deserves everything that his success has brought to him.

INTRODUCTION

On the one hand, this is a very personal memoir. It's the story of my career in bookmaking, with lots of stories that give you a flavour of what it was like to build a betting-shop empire. I'll tell you about some of the friends I made along the way, and one or two enemies! But as well as being a very personal book, I hope there's more than enough in here to entertain you...

If you've ever set foot in a betting shop, this book is for you. If you've ever had a big bet and lost, and thought to yourself *those greedy bookmaker bastards always win*, this book is definitely for you! If you grew up in the 1950s and 1960s, there's plenty in here that will be familiar to you.

I'm going to tell you about my life as a bookmaker, both in betting shops and on racetracks. But this story really is as much about the people I shared my working life with – the friends and punters that came along for the ride. The people who helped me. The people who made me laugh.

While I'm still waiting for the definitive television sitcom of the life and laughs of a 1970s betting shop, this will have to do. I've certainly had a lot of adventures along the way, and you'll read about some of them in this book. There have been some sad times too – and because even a bookmaker loses sometimes, you'll read about them as well.

Throughout this book, you'll notice that I mention a lot of people who have died. Many of them have sadly died from cancer. Some of them died quite recently, some of them died a long time ago. But they all lost their lives much too soon. A minimum of 20% of the net profits from this book will be donated to Marie Curie.

So if you want to help towards that cause too, then that's the best reason of all why this book is for you.

CHAPTER ONE

UNDER STARTER'S ORDERS

As a bookmaker, I've never taken odds on anything so unlikely, but in case you're interested, the odds are about 400 trillion to one against any of us ever being born...

I defied the odds, and was born on 13 March 1947 in Warrington hospital. I was the first child of Leonard and Kathleen. I remember the cobbled streets and chimney pots, and the sounds and smells of life back then. It was a way of life that doesn't exist anymore; we didn't even have a bathroom. We had to take baths every Sunday night in front of the fire. My dad worked in the local saw mill, earning £8 a week, and my mum worked in the cinema. Our extended family all lived in close proximity, and I loved the feeling of being part of a close-knit community.

Mum was pregnant again four years after I was born, and gave birth to my sister – Helen – who sadly died shortly after she was born. We used to go to Helen's grave, but we never really talked about her loss, it was just too painful for my mother to hear her name. Mum was thirty-one at the time, and she lived for the next fifty-two years with a broken heart.

My mother was a marvellous person, and she gave me everything I wanted. (I was a spoiled brat, really!) But she wasn't a lucky person; I think that's because she gave all her luck to me. I'm a firm believer that you make your own luck in life, but to be successful –

which I have been – you need a little bit extra. I do believe she gave me the extra luck that helped me on my way, and as I grew up, my mother's luck grew with me.

My mum was very religious, she never missed going to church, twice on Sundays. She often begged me to go with her, but somehow I always seemed to get a headache or a sore throat and wriggled out of it. (Now I'm a little bit older, I have started to think that I might just take her up on the offer of going to church a bit more, even though I'm about seventy years late!)

When I was about ten, my mum did manage to get me into the church choir at St John's Church in Earlestown. God knows how, but I got in! I don't think it was my singing voice that did it; my mum was friendly with the vicar and he didn't dare turn her down. My mum made friends easily, she seemed to know everyone in Earlestown, and everyone had good things to say about her. I hope that she passed a little bit of that easy way with people on to me too.

So I joined the choir, and I knew all the words to the hymns, but I didn't want to ruin the performance, so when we performed, I used to mime all the words. I think the vicar knew full well what was going on, but, of course, I never told my mother. She thought I was singing sweetly.

My relationship with my dad deteriorated in later life. He could be a selfish man, stubborn. But growing up, he was just Dad – and he was a man of his time. When I was still at primary school, he hit me with his belt, but it was the one and only time. I know I'd done something naughty although I can't remember just how naughty young Ron had been. I do remember he told me to go upstairs and take my trousers down so he could give me a good hiding.

Afterwards, I went straight round to my mother's parents' house to tell Grandad what had happened. I was still crying, and he simply said, "Stay here." He went over to see my dad and said, "Touch him again and you'll have me to answer to!" My dad never did hit me again after that!

I was one of five grandchildren. (There would have been six of us if Helen had lived.) As far as my grandparents were concerned, I was

8

the blue-eyed boy. They were lovely, and I was never out of their house. My grandfather took me to watch rugby league matches. I loved going with him there and back on the train. My very first job was programme seller at Warrington Rugby League when I was about thirteen. Ten minutes after kick-off, I packed my programmes up, cashed in, and went to join Grandad to watch the rest of the match, free of charge.

I got a lot of parenting from my grandad. I know my dad wasn't a bad man – he had a good heart – but he wasn't there to be my friend; he was there to make sure I grew up strong. He was certainly mad on horse racing, so I've got that to thank him for.

Dad would never go abroad, he just refused to set foot on a plane. Later in life, as a proud grandparent himself – he wouldn't even get on a plane to Majorca with my kids when my mum took them on holiday. As his life went on, he became more and more set in his ways. He'd go up the street, put his bet on in the betting shop, then go home and watch the races on TV. That was his day, and that was how he liked it.

My dad was from near Leicester, and the day I took my eleven-plus exam, Everton were playing Leicester at Goodison Park. He wanted to go and cheer on the Foxes, and I wanted to go because my team at the time was Everton. Everton had the best of the game, but Leicester won 1–0, and Dad was delighted. There were crowds of up to 75,000 in those days, and whenever I went to Goodison, I used to try to stand as near to the front as I could, so I could catch the eye of the toffee lady.

I should point out that when I moved to work in Manchester in 1967, I switched allegiance to Manchester City – and just in time too. In '68, they won the league. In '69 they won the cup, and I've been a City fan ever since. I took my two boys to Maine Road, and David has remained faithful, but Colin is a Liverpool fan. We'll move swiftly on!

Sport has always played a big part in my life, and I was certainly competitive from an early age. I liked to win, no matter what the cost...

I remember one particular school athletics tournament... My distance was 880 yards – I never lost a race over half a mile. My school house was Nansen. Our biggest rivals were Grenfell – they always seemed to win all the competitions. We were in the 880 race and I was third coming in off the second last band. There were two boys ahead of me, both Grenfell, and one of them was the school bully, Turnbull.

We came into the last bend, and I knew I could pass them any time I wanted and win by five yards. I'm breathing down their necks and Turnbull says, "Pass us and I'll kill you!" So I thought, *Right, I'll take a note of that!*

Coming off the last bend, I couldn't go on the inside. Turnbull had it covered. And his housemate, Armstrong, was side by side with him. I made to go outside them, but Armstrong moved into lane three to try and block me. And as he drifted over, I nipped in between them and passed them with ease. When I got to the finish line, I just kept running! I wasn't really a coward – just a bit clever. And I've been clever all my life!

I've only ever had two fights in my life – and I lost them both. The first time, I was about fourteen and my mum had gone off to the pub. My mum didn't drink and never normally went to the pub on a Saturday night. I was out with two of my pals, and we were annoying an old lady at the fish and chip shop. We kept opening the door and not going in. We didn't want to go in – the food was terrible! So, every time, she had to come round from behind the counter and close the door to keep the heat in. Little did I know that she had a guy called Keith Mills round the back – he was already the local hard case at seventeen years old – and all of a sudden, he appeared. I looked at my mates and said, "Come on, there's three of us..." All of a sudden, there was one – they'd both scarpered!

My mum and dad came home from the pub to find me lying on the sofa, blood everywhere, my nose twisted and turned. My mum thought we'd been burgled. I told her I'd been beaten up, and she looked at my dad and said, "I am never going out to the pub with you again!"

One of the names that stands out from my school days is David Paul Hughes. Now, I'm going to make a few diversions into the world of sport in this book, and here's the first: David went on to be captain of Lancashire County Cricket Club. We went through school together, all the way up to sixteen. In my first year of sixth form, I was made the school cricket captain, playing with boys who were one or two years older than me, and David was my vice captain. David is famous now for his exploits in the 1971 Gillette Cup semi-final. It was the 56th over, and getting dark, and David hit Johnny Mortimore for 24 off 1 over to seal their place in the final. It was a glittering Lancashire line-up with the likes of Clive Lloyd, Graham Fowler, Jack Simmons, and the Peters, Lee and Lever.

I started off as an opening bat, and made a fifty in my maiden first team appearance, aged fifteen. It was the worst fifty you've ever seen in your life – I played and missed more than I hit the ball! We were playing a Manchester-based team, Monton, and they had a quick left-arm bowler who represented the league side. And he really was quick. I was on fifty and he got me out LBW. (I was never out in a million years!) It pitched off stump and it clipped my pad going six inches wide of the off stump. I only ever scored one hundred. I was dropped three times before I was fifty, and then the second fifty was faultless.

I played league cricket for a few years, but stopped when I got into the bookmaking game. I kept my eye in, and carried on playing friendlies on Sundays. Then I returned to league cricket – at the same club – when I was twenty-three. Within a year, I was made club captain. We had a very good side.

I could still have opened the batting but I thought it was too much responsibility to be captain and opening bat. So I relegated myself to number eight and I became first change bowler. We were very successful and beat some of the top sides. A team called St Helens who had won the League four times in the previous six years. I played one of the best matches of my life at their ground; I can even still remember the score. It was the last match of the season. They came into the match having already won the league the week before.

The St Helens captain was notorious for putting teams in to bat. They had two very, very good opening bowlers. They used to get 130 wickets a season between them. One bowled big in dippers, and the other one moved it about off the pitch.

Their captain won the toss and I said, "You don't need to tell me! We're batting." We were a bit low on numbers, so our two opening bats were second team openers. And as the opening bats were walking out, my strike bowler, Tommy Hamilton, said, "Ron, I've got to go home, I forgot my boots." He was only going to bat at number ten so I sent him home to get them. (Tommy was just forty-nine when he died; cancer.) He was gone about an hour, and by the time he came back, the score board showed that we were one run for one wicket! I'd just told the batsmen to see the opening bowlers off, and they took me at my word.

After three hours, they bowled us out for 63. I was out for a duck, caught at short leg off a Dave Brighouse in-dipper. Towards the end of our innings, you could see the top of the wicket was going. It had rained that week and the surface was soft.

We had a bowler called John Appleton – another one who's dead from cancer – and he got figures of 8 for 22 that day. He was only medium pace. On a hard wicket, he was easy prey for a good batsman, but on that day, and on that wicket... If he could have folded up that wicket and taken it with him to every match he played, he would have got 8 for 22 every time he played!

Tommy had got one wicket, and I'd bowled three overs myself and they were all maidens. So we had them on nine wickets and there was one over to go when I brought Tommy back into the attack. Dave Brighouse – their seamer – was facing strike, and as I signalled the change of bowler, he said in his broad Lancastrian accent, "Thou can't put him on now, it's going dark." Calm as anything I said, "How do you know what he's going to bloody bowl?"

One of my players, Brian Carter, who was as placid as placid can be, stood up to Brighouse and said, "Stand up and face, you fucking coward!" So I tossed the ball to Tommy and said, "You've got one ball; he's going to appeal against the light." Tommy came in and cartwheeled his leg stump. You'd have thought that we'd won the World Cup!

We had another memorable match when we played Timperley in the Manchester Association Cup. The previous season, they'd won the Lancashire Knock-Out, so we knew we were in for a tough game. We played them at their home ground, and they batted first. Their opening bat was a guy called David Herd who had been centre forward for Manchester United and Arsenal. He was a good batsman, totally unorthodox, a bit of a cow-shotter. But if you put in a bad ball, he'd swish it away for four runs. He had no respect for pace bowlers. It didn't matter how quick they bowled, if they bowled a bad ball, or pitched it too short, he'd have it. He had a magnificent eye.

But I had an ace up my sleeve: a Derek Underwood type bowler; a guy called David Holmes. He died at just sixty years of age: cancer. By this time, I was batting at number eight because I wanted to concentrate on the captaincy. I knew I had seven good batsmen who were equally as good, if not better than me at numbers one to seven, and I really wanted to bowl. I routinely got my thirty wickets a season, and even managed to clean bowl quite a few good batsmen.

So Herd was on strike, and I threw the ball to David Holmes, who was a military medium left-arm over, pitching middle and leg. Herd was used to the quick stuff, he didn't know what to do with the slower balls he knew he was going to get from David, and Holmes duly clean bowled him third ball. He stood there looking at the pitch, wondering what had happened. But David had been clever and varied his pace, so after a slow ball, he surprised him with a quicker delivery, and then nobbled him with another slower ball.

They had another top batsman – Nigel Wood came in at number three. He was a left hander and David clean bowled him as well. That was both their top batsmen out for ducks. We beat them by six wickets in the end, and we all went to an Indian restaurant afterwards to celebrate.[1] Those little triumphs mattered, they helped bond the team. And we all felt very convivial towards each other when we staggered back to our homes at two in the morning! Like I said, I had always been competitive, and I loved to win whatever sport I was playing.

13

I played a lot of rugby too, and the powers that be said I had 'unlimited potential'. I played my first game in the grammar school first team when I was fifteen, and I was up against seventeen-year-olds. That was some debut!

I had been playing out half for the school second team, but when I was promoted to the first team, the coach put me in as a centre. I was the playmaker, the brains of the outfit. I had a good kick on me as well – I could kick goals from the touchline. In my first match, we were playing Liverpool Collegiate at home. Although I had plenty of faith in my own abilities, I was worried that I might be out of my depth in the first team. Even walking out onto the pitch, I wasn't sure I was ready, and I looked up to see the centre opposite me, and he was a man-mountain! Colin Massey – our other centre – looked up at his opposite man and he was a bloody midget! It did cross my mind to suggest we should swap, but I knew if I did that, everyone would mark me out as a coward.

We hadn't been playing long when the man-mountain got the ball and was charging towards me. There was only one thought in my mind: I had to bring him down. So I went for his legs but I missed him, and he charged straight through me and scored a try. After that, I just wanted to crawl into a hole and die. But the referee – Frank Holdsworth – who had played scrum half for Lancashire, and was the games master at our school had a quiet word in my ear. He said, "You'll have to do better than that, Wadey. You know he's only going to come at you again..."

I said, "He won't score again, sir!"

The next time he came at me, I was ready for him. Never mind trying to take his legs, I went straight for his jaw and stiff-armed him. He went up in the air, did a somersault, and came down with a bang. They had to bring on the smelling salts to bring him round. My moment of victory was short-lived. Frank reached for his whistle and I was sent off. But I was outraged. "You told me to stop him!" I said.

By the time I got to the dressing room, the adrenalin had died down and I was thinking, *He's a big bugger... I think I'll go home now!*

I didn't bother getting changed, I shoved my school blazer and trousers in my bag, got on my bike and pedalled as hard as I could all the way home before the match had finished!

The young Ron Wadey was nothing if not resourceful, and my survival instinct was kicking into gear too. I could handle myself with a bit of the rough stuff, but I was finding out that being a bit quicker and cleverer than my peers would serve me better in the long run than sheer brute strength. And so it proved...

1 I have a few more cricketing memories. I bowled Derek Randall out once! I'm quite proud of that. Decent player, and what a fielder that man was.

We were playing at Clumber park in Nottinghamshire, and I didn't even know Randall was playing. They were a couple of wickets down, and all of a sudden this bloke came out to bat, and I did a double take. "Jesus, it's Derek Randall!"

He was a bag of nerves at the crease, he kept hopping about, tapping the wicket; he just could not stand still. And there he was, sitting pretty on 73, easing towards a century, and he mistimed his shot. He didn't quite get over it, and I had caught him in the covers. I'm not sure if he'll remember that day in Clumber Park.

CHAPTER TWO

FALLING AT THE FIRST HURDLE

I left school at Christmas in the first year of sixth form. I was doing geography and English language as well, but the only subject I was really any good at was maths. I enjoyed that, and I had an aptitude for it. But by then, I'd discovered girls... And I loved girls, but if anything, I loved sport more. I didn't like cricket, I loved it, and I loved rugby most of all.

There were other distractions too. I'd started going out and having pints with my mates. We were just about old enough to get served in a pub then. I remember one time when six of us went to the Cavern Club in Liverpool, where The Beatles had been discovered. But our first port of call was a pub called The Grapes, opposite the Cavern Club.

We were all underage, and we were all paying for our own drinks. So the six of us went up to the bar and each ordered our own pint with our own money. One chap, Dougie Owen, who played scrum half for the school second team was a bit small in stature, and he was at the back of the queue. By the time he got to the bar, and we'd all got our drinks, he put on a gruff voice and said, "Pint of bitter, please." The barman gave him one look and said, "I can't serve you a pint!" So Dougie said, "Oh... I'll have two halves then!" (He ended up with a Coke.)

On another occasion, I was walking six miles back home after a night out in a pub in Warrington with a pal. It was pitch black, and between us we decided it would be a good idea to take a shortcut through the fields. We had no idea what we were doing, but we made our merry way back in what we hoped was the right direction. When we came to a gate across a farmer's field, my pal toppled over and landed in a cowpat. I toppled over and landed right beside him in a nice patch of soft grass. He cursed his luck and I thanked mine!

My walking-everywhere days were nearly over though. My dad bought me a car when I was seventeen, after I passed my test at the second attempt. It was a bit of an old banger, but it got me about. I wasn't one of those boys who had any great interest in cars, not like my son David. I knew how to open the door, and put the key in the ignition, but that was about it! So my dad impressed upon me that I had to check the oil regularly, and check the water level in the radiator, and I listened without really taking it in. And then one day, I had to go back to Dad, my tail between my legs and say, "Dad, I've done something terrible... I've put engine oil in the radiator."

Needless to say, he wasn't too pleased, but he sorted out the car for me, while Mum set about helping me find gainful employment...

My mates had all left school after their O levels and got jobs, and they all had money. I could see them going out and having fun whenever they wanted, and I thought, *Hang on a minute, I want a bit of that*... So I left school, and full of enthusiasm set out to get a job. In the end, my mum got a job for me; it was her social network coming to the rescue again! She knew the head cashier at T&T Vickers who were biscuit machinery manufacturers. Of course she did; she knew *everyone*, and everyone liked her. So I got a job in the wages office, and it was dull as ditch water! I was on a full-time, five-days-a-week contract, but it was a two-day-a-week job, really. Employees got paid on a Friday. So you calculated everyone's tax and insurance contributions on a Thursday. The boss went to the bank for the cash on a Friday morning, and then we put it in envelopes with wage slips, and the workers formed an orderly queue. That was all there was to it; I was bored out of my head.

I was on £3 a week, and I paid that to my mother. But then I'd go and ask her for a pound back, and sooner or later, I'd wrangled the whole three quid out of her! She was a soft touch where I was concerned.

So I was cruising in my job, and finally had a bit of money in my pocket, but I was already looking for something else... A calling?! Not far from the factory was a betting shop, and because of my dad, I already had a healthy interest in horse racing. My dad was a marvellous punter. He'd tell you why a particular horse was going to win... and then after the race, he'd tell you exactly why it didn't win!

So I was intrigued by the betting shop. My dad had never actually taken me with him to place a bet because I'd been too young, but now I was (just about) old enough, and would have looked older through the smoke! It was a slightly magical place. The fug of cigarette smoke and the chatter of excited punters filled the air. It wasn't like anywhere I'd been before, and it was a world away from the wages office.

I started popping into the shop whenever I could. I placed a few small bets – just two shillings each way – but it wasn't the betting that interested me. I was fascinated by the mechanics of it – the odds and the forecasts, the calculations the bookies were making, and the fact that, whatever happened, the bookmaker always seemed to win in the end. I'd found my calling alright!

Then one day, the head cashier caught me in the betting shop when I should have been in the office. I got a warning that day. But then he found me in there twice more. The cheeky beggar followed me in that last time and tapped me on the shoulder. "What are you doing in here?" he said. I thought it was pretty obvious what I was doing in there! "I'm having a bet," I said. "That's what this place is for." He didn't look happy. "Besides," I said, "I'm on my break." (By then, I think I was on about three breaks an hour!) But it was third time unlucky for me, and I was sacked on the spot.

In those days, you could get sacked from one job on a Wednesday – like I did – and start a new job the following Monday – like I did! I started as a trainee buyer at UKAEA, which was, potentially, far more interesting than being a wages clerk. But there was a problem. The head buyer didn't know what he was doing, and I didn't respect him at all. There was an even bigger problem though – I knew that job wasn't for me either.

But at least I had my rugby to fall back on...

After school, I'd joined the local rugby club's Colts team, and it was a really good team. I played centre. The captain was Franny Cotton. He was like three players in one, and went on to play prop forward for England. There was another lad in the team called David Hill, who went on to sign a professional contract with Wigan, with his elder brother, Cliff. David was a magnificent playmaker, and he made so many tries for me. All I had to do was catch the ball, and I'd be on his shoulder, waiting for the gap. I could score two or three tries like that every match.

We were being coached by Don Gullick, who had played rugby union for Wales. He was a great coach, and I like to think he knew I was a good player. I had a fantastic side-step, and a powerful hand-off. (And I could punch as well if need be!) The talent was there, and everyone told me I was going to be a county player, but I was immature. I was lazy. And I just couldn't be bothered with training. Don used to tell me, "You could be a yard faster if you put the effort in." But I didn't listen. Maybe I thought my talent would pull me through. Maybe I thought I'd just get lucky, but my mother's luck hadn't quite caught up with me yet.

We played against Orrell, the top club in the area at the time. Before the kick-off, David called me over and said, "You see their centre? He's a county player for Lancashire."

I played it cool. "Oh yeah? When's the next county match then?"

"Next week."

"Well he won't be playing!"

And when he came at me, I let him have it. Discreetly, of course! He passed the ball and I just put my arm round him and brought him down, 'my way'. At least this time, I wasn't spotted and sent off, and he never came near me again after that. (I think he did make it to his next county match, even after his tangle with me!)

That game was an absolute bloodbath. Ian Fearnley, our full back, got concussed but wouldn't go off, so he had to go and play on the wing. He couldn't even see the ball after that, never mind catch it. We were losing 8–6, and I got the ball, pushed their man to one side, and broke through. I had the full back to beat. I knew Ian was on the wing, and as I looked to pass it to him, he turned around and started walking the other way! So I got flattened for my trouble, and we missed a golden scoring opportunity. But with three minutes left, I got the ball twenty yards out in front of their posts and dropped a goal: 9–8 to us. We won the match.

We were all happy in the changing room afterwards, and Gullick patted me on the back. "Great goal, Ron."

"Well you know what they say, don't you, Mr Gullick..." He looked confused. So I told him, "The match is never over until the unfit centre drops the goal!" He wasn't one for smiling, but he smiled at that.

I kept my place in the team anyway, and I was one of seven players picked for a seven-aside tournament at Oxford University. It was a 64-team knockout, and we got to the last eight against Kidderminster. We beat Kidderminster to reach the semi-finals, but we finished with six men. Don't worry, I didn't get sent off and let the side down! But I did get badly injured. My leg slipped out from under me as I was collecting the ball and I broke my ankle.

So I ended up in hospital. There weren't any substitutes, so our six men lost against the seven men of Widnes. There was only ever going to be one winner. In the end, we only lost by a couple of points. With seven men, we'd have won it. And that put paid to my 'promising' rugby career. While I hadn't been pinning my future hopes on a glittering career as a county rugby player, that time off did give me the chance to think about what I did want to do.

I was off work from UKAEA for eight weeks after that, and it gave me plenty of opportunity to read the job adverts. I would hobble out to the local betting shop on my crutches and read the adverts in *The Sporting Life*. And two adverts caught my eye. The first: 'Trainee Betting Shop Manager required in Wigan'. It was at a shop owned by Wally Mills who had a dozen shops, spread out over the North West. So I rang him, gave him my qualifications, and told him maths was my best subject. I added that I couldn't go in for a job interview because I'd broken my leg. And he said, "Well, I can't give you a job either, because you're not eighteen!"

I was only a month off eighteen, so he said to ring him again when I was able to walk, and he'd give me an interview. I went on my crutches, talked the talk, and he offered me the job there and then. But then there was the other advert that had caught my eye: The world champion boxer Terry Downes had retired and gone into bookmaking in London. He had built up a nice string of betting shops, and he was advertising for trainee managers. I thought, *I fancy London...* I spoke to Terry, and in his broad Cockney accent, he said, "I like the sound of your voice, son. Consider yourself 90% hired. But I want to see you. Get on a train to London, I'll pay your fare. I'll buy you a bit of lunch too."

I told my dad, and he was elated. I told my mum, and she started crying. Seeing my mum cry nearly broke my heart, and I knew I couldn't leave her and move to London. I rang Mr Downes back, and told him I couldn't meet him. Then I took the job in Wigan. I came off the crutches and went straight to work in Wally's Wigan shop, and took to it like a duck to water. Wally taught me all the formulas that I needed to learn, and I picked it up just like that. Within six months, I was running a shop for him.

The odds came easily to me, and I had a good relationship with the punters. I was my mother's son, after all. I had a good relationship with a young lady called Catherine, too. In fact, we got married. Catherine was already pregnant with my first son, David, when we walked down the aisle.

I was doing well in the betting shop, but we didn't have a lavish life, and we didn't even have anywhere to live at first. So after the wedding, we moved in with Catherine's mother. That was a struggle! I'd loved going home to my mother's cooking, she was a wonderful cook; Catherine's mum wasn't! I got cheese on toast for my tea about five times a week!

I learned my trade in Wigan and I stayed there for a couple of years, until I saw an advert for a job at a Mark Lane betting shop in

Manchester, offering a fiver a week more. I'd only been getting paid £20 a week, and with a wife and one child – then another one on the way – some extra money was going to be very useful. And there was the fact that I'd always wanted to work in a big city. If I couldn't have London, Manchester would do just fine.

So I moved to Manchester for the extra money, and the extra experience, and although I already felt as if I knew my stuff, it turned out that I still had a lot to learn...

You learn very early on in your life in bookmaking that you have to scrutinise any big bet very carefully before you can accept it. In some cases, it just isn't viable to take the bet, the implications of losing on it can be disastrous. Very early into my career at Mark Lane's there was a juvenile race for two-year-olds. Most of those horses would never have raced before, so the betting was all about the breeding. A horse from a good stallion or a good dam would always come in favourite to win a race like that. This was an eight-runner race, so for each way you would pay for first, second, and third. The favourite had odds of 2/5; it was practically a certainty. The second favourite was 4/1, and the third favourite was 10/1.

I knew full well that if the 4/1 chance finished first, second or third, the punter was at least going to get his money back. If he had a tenner each way, and the horse finished second at 4/1 – that represented a quarter of the odds. (That's evens in other words.) The punter could place a tenner on an each-way bet for a total bet of £20, and his return would have been £20. That's basically a free-win bet, and it wouldn't have been viable for us to take it on.

So that day, a guy came in that I'd never seen before. He was a cocky so-and-so in his tinted glasses, and he said he wanted to make a bet on the two-year-old race – £500 each way on the second favourite at 4/1.

I said, "No chance, mate, I can't take this. You can have £500 for the win, £250 a place."

He put £1,000 on the counter. "Take the bet."

I shook my head. "It's not worth my job."

He was getting angry. "£500 each way... take the fucking bet!"

I stood fast. "No, sir."

He looked me in the eye and said, "Mark my words, if this horse wins, you'll be in Salford Royal Infirmary this evening."

"No bet."

He stayed in the shop and watched the race. And I was watching him, watching the race. When it was over, he looked over, pointed and said, "You're a lucky man!" and walked out. His horse had finished second!

I was still a bit green as far as city-centre activities were concerned, and I didn't have a clue who he was. But it turns out he was Jimmy Donnelly – Jimmy the Weed as he was known – one of the Quality Street Gang; the Manchester Mafia. That song 'The Boys are Back in Town'? That's about them, they say. If he'd wanted me in Salford Royal Infirmary that evening, he would have made it happen, no question.

I didn't run into the Quality Street Gang again after that. I assume they found a different betting shop where the staff were more easily intimidated. And I had a good time in Manchester, but for one other thing: I didn't get on with the area manager, Peter, and he didn't get on with me. I've always been a bit forthright; I've always been one to speak my mind, and he didn't like that one bit.

I thought he was a bit of an imposter. The odds didn't come easily for him as they did for me. He didn't have any kind of rapport with the customers. He was in a cushy job and winging it, really. So I didn't make it easy for him. Maybe I was arrogant, but I knew that I was doing a good job in the shop, and I knew the upper echelons didn't want to lose me, never mind what the area manager might have thought about me.

So, because I knew what I was doing, they moved me from the High Street shop to the main shop on Cateaton Street, next to Manchester cathedral. Now, it would have been quicker and easier for me to travel to work on the train, but I'd got myself a car of my own, and I liked to use it! Unfortunately, I never allowed for traffic, and consequently I was regularly ten minutes late getting to work. I was supposed to get there at 9:30 a.m. with a view to opening the shop at 10:00 a.m., but I never quite made it.

I had to drive past the shop to park the car, and I was driving past the shop one day, ten minutes late as usual, when who should I see on the door step but my area manager. He clocked me driving past straightaway, so I thought I might as well give him something to get really angry about. I was already ten minutes late, I thought I might as well make it fifteen. I was going to get bollocked either way. So I drove round the block another couple of times.

When I finally arrived and went in, he said, "I saw you drive past fifteen minutes ago. Where have you been?" I told him I hadn't been able to find a parking spot. Perhaps he knew I'd done it to wind him up. So he said, "This has got to stop. If it doesn't, you're on your bike." It was a fair cop, so I said something to defuse the situation, but I already knew I was on my way out of there.

I'd made friends with a bloke called Steve Mallinson, who worked for a bookmaker called Ernie Peters. Peters had a dozen or so shops in Manchester and Blackpool, and they had a shop around the corner from Mark Lane's High Street shop – they were my main competition. It was a good shop, right outside Smithfield Market, and the market traders used to go in and have a flutter. In those days, the city-centre shops would take some pretty big bets. A thousand-pound bet was a pretty regular occurrence.

I'd met Steve and a few of the other local bookmaking staff in the pub next to the betting shop on the High Street. It was all shop talk – How many bets have you taken today? Any big bets? I was young, but Steve could already see that I knew what I was doing. I had never been a serious punter, but the other guys were. I've had the odd bet, here and there, and put a couple of quid on the football coupon in their shop, but I was already a firm believer that there are two sides of the fence, and you can only be on one side. You can't be on both.

Steve was definitely a punter. I knew he was earning about the same as me, £25–£30 a week, but he came into my shop every day and placed bets. His daily outlay would be around a hundred quid, so I thought, *Where's he getting his money from?* It turned out the general manager was his brother-in-law, Les Churm, who worked in the same shop. Peter Done managed a shop for Ernie Peters, as did his uncle, Eric Done. And a name you'll know – Fred Done – who now trades as Betfred with 1,500 betting shops – was the manager of another one. They would all have been earning about thirty quid a week – the same as me – and they all lived in expensive houses in Worsley. I thought, *There must be something in this bookmaking business!*

So one day when Steve came in to make a bet, I asked if there were any jobs going at Ernie Peters. He told me to leave it with him. He was back at the end of the day saying that a mate of his, and his brother, had left Ernie Peters to set up a couple of betting shops in Salford, and they were buying a third. "It's Fred Done," he told me. "He's got big ambitions... He's asked me to ask you to go and meet him at his office in Pendleton tonight."

So I went to meet Fred and Peter Done, and I got the job there and then. They'd been expecting someone capable, but they weren't expecting me! I really knew my stuff. They were impressed. Fred raised my salary and he said, "I'll tell you what, I'll throw a company car in as well." That was unheard of in those days. He asked if I was going to accept on those terms. I knew when I had a dead cert, and this was one of those times. How could I have said no?

But there was more. "Trust me," he said. "I am going places." And he was spot on, he has gone places. He said, "When we get big enough to justify having a general manager, that job is yours." I couldn't believe what he was offering me: more money, a car, and a promotion when the time was right. We shook hands. I was now working for Fred Done.

The new shop he had bought was near the docks at Salford. I built it up and increased the turnover. There's always a balance to strike in any betting shop between keeping the punters happy and keeping the takings high. But I pulled it off. Things were going well. Mostly... I did manage to crash my company car, and I don't think that went down too well.

Then, about six months later, Peter walked in with a bald-headed guy; it was Les Churm, the general manager at Ernie Peters. Peter said they'd bought another couple of shops, and introduced me to Les. I was friendly. At first. I told Les that I already knew him, and our paths had crossed a few times. I said I'd been working around the corner from him for two years, and his brother-in-law used to come into my shop for a bet every day. Les was friendly too. But then Peter went on, "Ron, I want you to get to know Les very well, he's our new general manager." You could have knocked me over with a feather. I gave it a second or two, then said, as calm as you like, "Can I have a word, Pete? In private?" He knew.

We went into the back office. I was livid. I said, "That was supposed to be my job. You know that."

Peter tried to fob me off. "But Les has got more experience. He's been general manager at Ernie Peters – a twelve-shop chain. You haven't got that experience."

I didn't want to hear it. "Your brother promised me that job. But now, you've crapped on me."

He didn't know what to say next. But I did. "There's the keys," I told him.

"Ron, Ron, no..." he started.

I wasn't in the mood to listen. "You've done the dirty on me. You know you have. Send me the money you owe me in the post. I'm off!" I had lost all respect for them. Fred wasn't the only ambitious one. I was ambitious too, but I had been stopped in my tracks. Suddenly I'd gone from being the bright young thing to being cast aside, and I felt as if I had no future ahead of me.

Stuff them all anyway! That's when I decided to resurrect my cricket career. I didn't care about having a career in bookmaking anymore, I abandoned my long-term plans. I would be happy with a nine-to-five, Monday-to-Friday job, and play cricket at the weekend. So I got a job at Tarmac Construction in the accounts department. It felt like I'd gone back to work at the biscuit factory, but I just treated it as a job to fill the time and pay the bills.

For a while, the cricket came first. I was playing for Earlestown, and I remember one game in particular. We were riding high after beating Prescot at home. Naturally, we had a few victory pints in the club bar, and to show there were no hard feelings, my friend, the Prescot captain, Bob Mawdsley, was with us. The banter was relentless, and at around five or six pints in, one of my teammates, Colin Wakefield, piped up, "You know what your problem is, don't you, Ron?"

"No," I replied wearily, "but I'm sure you're going to tell me."

"You're too slow in the field," he stated, a note of challenge in his voice.

I wasn't having that. I was the fastest outfielder in that team, and he knew it. I threw down the gauntlet...

"Do you fancy a race then, Colin? One lap of the cricket pitch, loser buys the next round."

It's one thing dishing out the banter, but then you've got to be able to take it. Fortunately, Colin wasn't a man to back down from a challenge. The race was on, but only after we'd each downed our sixth pint, obviously!

Colin took the early lead, but I had plenty in reserve to overtake him anytime I wanted. I let him enjoy his lead right up to the final 25 yards, then eased in front. I was a couple of strides ahead at the line, turned to Colin and said, "I'll see you in the bar, mine's a pint."

Colin bought the next round. And I'm glad to say that we're still friends to this day. (We don't race as much as we used to though!)

From the vantage point of the club bar, life looked good enough. I was twenty-seven years old, and enjoying life where I could. I was playing my cricket, but going through the motions at work, and things weren't too good at home either. I split up from Catherine; I'm afraid, I'd been a naughty boy, and we went our separate ways. The boys were nine and eight years old at the time.

I left her and spent as much time as I could with the real love of my life back then – cricket. But if my break-up with Catherine was bad, worse was to follow. I had a bust-up at the cricket ground! The club wasn't really progressing as much as I thought it should have, and I was typically vocal about what changes they should make. It didn't go down too well. I made up my mind to leave, and that was the end of another relationship.

I had some rebuilding to do. I met another woman – Maureen – with whom I had my lovely daughter, Michelle. Then I found another cricket team; I played for Flixton Cricket Club for a couple of years. I got on well enough with the captain – and he used me as a middle order bat and a change bowler – but my face didn't really fit at Flixton. I never even got a fifty. I was run out on forty-nine a couple of times. Once was my fault. The other time, I gave the guy a good bollocking for running me out.

But I was starting to feel like my life was stuck on forty-nine. I'd gone from a good income to a pittance, and I was always skint. I'd lost full-time care of my kids; I knew I needed to do something else with my life, and the only other thing I knew was bookmaking...

CHAPTER THREE

BACK IN THE SADDLE

It was 1975, and I was twenty-eight years old. In concert venues and on the streets of England, angry young men were making the news. By that stage I was, if not an angry young man, a man on a mission, and I had a plan...

There was a betting shop in Newton le Willows – part of Earlestown – up for sale. Alf Blake was the property owner and the bookmaker. Alf was a big rough-and-ready fella; we'd seen each other around and about, and I knew that Alf had a problem... He lived in Oldham, a good forty minutes' drive from his shop. "How much do you want for your shop, Alf?" He said he wanted £1,300 for it. He would have asked for more he said, but admitted it wasn't doing good business, and he was going to retain the premises. It didn't bother me too much that the shop was struggling, I knew I could turn it around. And what Alf didn't know was that I wasn't just interested in *his* shop. I had bigger designs. Like I said, I was ambitious.

Alf's shop was on the end of a row of about six terraced houses, with a pub next door. That was back in the days when a betting shop and a pub went cap in hand. On the other side of the main road there was a big factory, and a quarter of a mile further up the road, there was a Labour Club. In the Labour Club car park there was a second betting shop. Keith Davies, an independent bookie was the owner. If you had any money left in your pocket after vising those two, you could take a right turn onto another row of shops on Park Road, and you'd find a third betting shop. These three shops were all within a radius of a quarter of a mile, and I wanted them all.

I was averaging one and a half grand a week turnover after my first two weeks, and I estimated that the shop on Park Road was doing the same. But Keith Davies' was the pick of the three. His punters didn't just have car parking, they had the Labour Club next door. It was perfect. Keith's shop must have been taking at least three grand a week, I reckoned. So that whole quarter of a mile radius was taking six grand a week. If you had a few betting shops taking £6,000 pounds a week in those days, you had a gold mine. Compared with today, the overheads were nothing. Keith's shop was definitely the jewel in the crown, the shop I coveted most of all. And I made myself a promise that one day I was going to buy that shop.

A few weeks into life at the shop, it was all ticking over nicely. I was playing it very carefully. I didn't have any big liabilities. I paid the asking price for the shop, although Alf retained the property, and I was paying a small rent of about £20 a week. It was a pokey shop, I'll admit it, just one room of a terraced house, effectively. The area of the first floor was probably only 200 square feet. You couldn't have swung a cat around in there. But none of that mattered. I'd gone from being a hired hand in someone else's shop to being out of the game altogether, to having my own shop. I was back, and I had an empire to build.

Two or three weeks in, I had a visitor. The day's horses had finished, and the shop should have been closed, but I was still working in Manchester time, where they stayed open to take bets on the dog racing until 6.30 p.m. I was doing everything I could to drum up trade and eke out as much profit as I could. If I could have taken one £5 bet on a dog at Belle Vue, I'd have been happy, so when the door opened and this chap stepped in, I assumed he'd come to put a bet on a dog. As it turned out, he had an altogether different mission in mind. I didn't know who he was but he had done his homework on me. He introduced himself as Norman, he was the owner of the Park Road shop. He knew a little bit about my history, and he knew I'd got the licence for the shop. I liked his directness. And then he said those magic words to me. "Are you ambitious, Ron?"

I said, *"Slightly!"*

So he said, "Do you want to buy my shop?"

At that, I locked the door, put the kettle on, and we settled down for a proper chat.

"I'd love to buy your shop, Norman," I started. "But I need money to buy your shop... and I haven't got any."

Norman said some more magic words. "I'm not bothered about the money."

It was a funny way to sell a shop! Norman was full of magical words, but he wasn't an idiot. He did want money for the shop, £1,400 in fact, but he was prepared to wait.

"Give me £200 now," he said, "and pay me £100 a month for twelve months and it's yours."

It was an unbelievable offer. At those numbers, the shop would pay for itself, and I'd be one step closer to having my monopoly – and my jewel in the crown. There was just one problem...

"Norman," I said, "I can't be in two places at once."

I had a lot to think about. But before he left, I wanted to know why Norman was selling. He replied a bit ruefully, "Because if I don't sell up, my wife is going to divorce me."

I was none the wiser.

"She's very religious," he said. "She thinks it's immoral that I'm making a living like this. I've got to sell it and get a 'proper' job."

I hadn't ever had any moral concerns over my career in bookmaking, and to this day, I still haven't. Maybe it's because of the way I ran the shops. In time, I came to know each and every returning customer that came in. For them, the trip to the betting shop was a part of their social life. I made sure they felt welcome, and I made sure the shops were nice places to be. At their height, they were full of friends and banter. People came in and had a little bet, but they also caught up with the craic, and, win or lose, they went home happier for having had a little bit of excitement in their day.

If I owned a pub, I'd be profiting in getting people drunk. If I had a newsagent's I'd be selling cigarettes to teenagers... And that's when I remembered my friend Ken Donegan. Ken had a newsagent's and supplied the newspapers for the betting shop I'd run for Fred Done. He used to come in and have a bet with us, and he always said to me, "Ron, I've always wanted to be a bookmaker. Do you ever fancy having a go at a partnership?"

Every time, I would give him a look and say, "I've got an ex-wife and two kids. I couldn't afford to do that, Ken!"

But just then, his parting words came back to me: "Well, if you're ever interested, you let me know..."

Even after I'd left it all behind, and was working at Tarmac, and playing my cricket at the weekends, I'd see Ken out and about, and he'd say, "Don't forget, Ron, don't forget." Well, the day had come. It was Ken's lucky day. I hurried off to look for his number and found it scribbled on the back of an old betting slip. Sure enough, Ken was still keen as mustard. I told him the partnership was on. He gave me £650 for his half, and another hundred quid for half of the £200 deposit. Going halves meant that I still had a few quid left to play with.

There were a few teething problems. Ken didn't know anything about running a betting shop, so I had to give him a few lessons. There were some dodgy moments when Ken would ring me from the other shop and ask questions like, "Ron, this guy backed a winner. It was a £10 bet on a 13/8, what do I pay him?"

"That'll be £26.25, Ken."

Then there'd be another call, and another, until I had to say, "Ken, wait until you've got three or four winners. These phone calls are costing us a bloody fortune!" He picked up the basics soon enough and then he'd only ring me if he had a double and a treble, for example. But we were off, and we were doing okay. Mostly...

Ken had some matrimonial problems. He was a good footballer and, like me, he got into trouble 'playing away from home'. In the end, he left his wife and went to live in Lancaster while he was still in partnership with me. But it was a bloody long way from Lancaster to the shop every day. He let his wife have the paper shop as part of the settlement, so financially he was stretched. They had three children together too, and suddenly, he was living beyond his means. At that point he understood why I hadn't wanted to jump into a partnership a few years earlier when I was newly separated.

But we kept ploughing on. I still had the same fiery ambition, but because of his problems, Ken didn't have the same passion for it anymore. He didn't have the same single-minded focus as me. For me, the ultimate target was that third shop – my jewel in the crown. And that is when my mother's luck struck...

We'd been in the two shops about a year, and we'd built the business up from doing around one and a half grand a week each to closer to two grand a week each. I was a local man, that helped. I had built up a good reputation and that gave the punters more reason to bet with me. Better that they put their 'hard earned' into a local man's shop, than into one of the many faceless, corporate-type betting shops that were springing up.

I didn't always get everything right, though. I took on some credit business on the telephone, and there are still some people who owe me money that I'll never get. (And yes, if you're one of those people and you're reading this, I haven't forgotten you!) But you show me one bookmaker who isn't owed money. I know of one of the big bookmakers who had to close the credit business because they were owed hundreds of thousands of pounds they were never going to get.

So I tried everything I could to push our profit margins higher. I was in that shop until all hours, I lived it and breathed it, but I didn't mind because I felt like we were moving steadily towards our goal. I still needed a little bit of my mother's luck though. A letter came through the post by recorded delivery. It was a compulsory purchase order from the council. The council wanted their land back – perhaps they thought three betting shops in a quarter of a mile was more than enough. Somebody put me in touch with a bloke in Wakefield who dealt with compulsory purchase orders, and he advised me to look at my last six months of trading and pick out the best six weeks. Whatever sum that came to would be the compensation I'd get before we were closed down.

We'd been doing very nicely thank you, and we got a tidy little sum. The bulldozers came in to knock down the first shop and the row of houses, but I didn't mind one bit. I wasn't ever sentimental about the bricks and mortar. We'd built up the basis of a good local business, the second shop was still taking a couple of thousand a week, and I could sell it on to anyone – just not to another bookmaker.

So with the dust in my hair, and armed with a substantial war chest, I went to see Keith Davies. The situation had changed, and I was going to make him an offer for his shop that he couldn't refuse. It was Advantage, Ron.

I waited until the last bets had been paid, and then made the short trip to Keith's shop. Bold as brass I went in and said, "Keith, I've come to buy your shop."

I think it's fair to say he hadn't been expecting that. "But the shop's not for sale..."

"Oh I think it is, Keith. Everything's for sale," I said. "I've got a damn good idea what your turnover is... I'll give you twenty grand for it." That didn't include the property, which was still owned by the Labour Club.

After the surprise had passed, I could tell that Keith was interested. He hadn't thrown me out on my ear, and he was still listening.

We talked a bit more and Keith's resolve was crumbling. I'm not going to say it's a vocation, but being a bookmaker is a job that takes over your life, and if you're not one hundred per cent committed to it, you're better off getting out of it. It looked to me as if Keith was ready to jump ship. Keith said he needed to speak to his wife. She was an equal partner in the business. I gave him my home number and didn't expect to hear from him for a day or two.

The phone rang later that evening. It was Keith. "Ron," he said, "we'll sell you the shop..." I started to thank him, when he stopped me in my tracks. "But the price is thirty grand!"

"Alright, Keith, I'll ring *you* back!"

I got on the phone to Ken. I knew the shop wasn't worth thirty grand to anybody else, and I couldn't even be sure it would be worth thirty to us. But it made sense. The three shops had been taking in a good six-to-eight thousand pounds per week before the compulsory purchase order came in, minus three sets of overheads. I was going to reduce the overheads by about 66% and bring all the punters in under one roof. It was a purpose-built betting shop, it had the car park, it had the footfall from the Labour Club bar, it was perfect. We weren't just buying one shop, we were buying the whole area.

There were times when I'd just stood over the road and watched punters cross the Labour Club car park after a pint, go in and make a bet, then go back to the club for another couple of pints; an hour later they'd pop back over and make another bet.

I said to Ken, "I've got to buy it." And he said he was in.

We couldn't give Keith the thirty grand upfront, or we'd have been skint all over again. In bookmaking, your stock is money. Ken was already struggling to make ends meet as it was, and we both drew £300 a week in wages. It was time to see the bank manager.

I'd always got on very well with my bank manager. I didn't borrow money, and I put plenty of money in. In banking terms I was a safe bet. But it had been a while, and the old manager had moved on. I met the new guy and explained the situation; I told him I needed a £5,000 overdraft. He didn't know me from Adam, but his secretary did, and as he looked over to her, she gave him a big thumbs up. That was good enough for him, and I got the overdraft.

The deal was done. I paid Keith the money, and I suspect we both left that day thinking we'd got the better end of the deal. After a couple of weeks of averaging £10,000 a week, we never looked back. We didn't need the overdraft after all. Kenron Racing was off to a flying start!

CHAPTER FOUR

KENRON RACING

It was the start of the Eighties. I'd been living with Maureen in Warrington for a few years, and Michelle was growing up fast. On Sundays, I used to go and play football with David and Colin, and we'd got out for trips together. I must have been doing something right as a father; they both still speak to me!

The Kenron business empire was growing. We bought a shop off Corals in St Helens, and I was always on the lookout for more. Fred Done had a shop nearby in Lowton, out on the ring road. It was a decent shop on a pub's car park. But at a punter-squeezing size of about 400 square feet, it was just too small for him. By then, Fred must have had about twenty shops, and the Lowton shop just didn't fit in with what he was trying to achieve. I liked the look of it though. I could see there was a lot of passing trade, and I knew I could do good things with it.

Fred put the shop up for sale, and I considered my options. We hadn't exactly parted on good terms, but I knew that if I wanted to get anywhere, I was going to have to let bygones be bygones. So I got on the phone to Fred, and he was as nice as pie. There wasn't any talk of crashed company cars (from him), or of broken promises (from me).

I looked at the numbers; the turnover was up and down. They had a few decent punters on the books, but they didn't seem to have the loyalty of a lot of regulars to call upon. One week they could take three or four thousand; the next week it could be just fifteen hundred. And from that point of view, it didn't seem like such a great investment...

But I wasn't discouraged. I bought the shop for eight grand, and within a month the big gamblers started coming back and more of the passing trade punters turned into regulars. There wasn't really any great secret to running a good bookmaker's, you just had to know how to keep your customers happy. You had to give them nice premises and treat them well. A betting shop in those days was a living, breathing place, and it was an important part of the community. It was like a pub. The regulars wanted to be treated right. They wanted to feel like they were known and appreciated.

The manager Fred had running the shop hadn't got a clue. I'd popped in a couple of times for a look around, and he didn't even speak to the customers. Maybe it was my mother's influence coming out in me, but I'd always instinctively known that, if you wanted to get any kind of customer loyalty, you relied on your charisma, and you made your customers feel welcome.

Plenty of bookmakers I knew struggled with a losing day. But to me, it was all part of the job. I knew that happy, winning punters would keep coming back. And invariably, the scales would balance out in my favour. So I let them enjoy their little moments of triumph, and I enjoyed the banter that came with the territory. Banter is the beating heart of the betting shop, and the bookmakers that can take it – as well as dish it out – are the ones that inspire the loyalty of their punters.

So we bought Fred's shop for eight grand, and in our first four weeks of trading, we made eight grand! I made a point of telling Fred when I saw him at Cheltenham races. (He was really happy to hear that, as you can probably imagine!)

Then we got a fourth shop in Warrington town centre. In the space of a few years, I'd gone from telling Norman that I couldn't be in two places at once to running four shops! I stayed at our 'head office' – the jewel in the crown next to the Labour Club – and we got staff in for the St Helens shop and Fred Done's old shop. Ken went to the Warrington shop; it was a decent shop, but it was bloody hard to make a profit in it – the punters were too shrewd!

Ken used to come back to the head office every night, and I said, "Any good?" Ken just shook his head. So I took a look at the bets and I kept seeing the same two sets of handwriting on the biggest wining bets. Every time there were big winners, the same two people were cashing in.

I said, "It's these two blokes, Ken, the same two, every time."

But Ken wasn't having it. "They're nice blokes, Ron," he said.

I couldn't care less if they were nice blokes or not, they were winning off us, hand over fist. They could have been Mahatma Gandhi and the Pope for all I cared. But Ken still couldn't see the problem.

"Look at the turnover..."

I told him, "You can't feed your kids on turnover, Ken!"

I knew we had to get rid. The Warrington shop was a bad apple, and it was eating into the profits of our other three shops, but Ken didn't like it. Things were getting strained between us. It wasn't helped by the fact that although we were 'equal' partners, the work wasn't been done on an equal footing. I was working late most evenings, and every Sunday, I had to do security work to make sure the managers of the other shops were doing everything by the book. Back in the early Eighties, betting shops made good percentages – maybe eight per cent more (gross) than they do today. And eight per cent of a lot of money is a lot of money! One of us had to make sure that everything was accounted for, and that was only ever going to be me.

That was when I met Frank Seymour, he was the Director of William Hill Northwestern. They had a shop in Warrington town centre, just around the corner from our shop, and I knew that if we closed our shop in Warrington, all our business would go to Hill's. So I did what I always did; I came right out and asked for what I wanted.

I went to meet with Frank just to get a sense of what I might be able to squeeze out of him in part exchange for our Warrington shop. We got on well, and we were both honest and upfront about what we wanted out of the other. As my luck would have it – or as my mother's luck would have it – he wanted us to close our shop to help his numbers, and he had a place in Upholland that he thought I might be interested in.

I did my usual due diligence on the shop and I saw that it was doing a similar turnover to our Warrington shop, but with a lot more tickets, and that was music to my ears. The smaller the bet in a betting shop, the higher the margin, and the higher the profitability. The guys who used to hit you hardest were the ones who came in and put a winning hundred-quid bet on at 5/1. They'd take their £500 and you'd never see them again.

I liked what I saw of the Upholland shop, but for one thing: the manager was a zombie. There were a lot of them about! This guy had no charisma, no relationship with the punters whatsoever, and I thought, *I'd be good in this shop*. I knew we had to shift Warrington – it wasn't working for us – and this felt like a good move at the right time.

So Frank offered us a straight swap: Warrington for Upholland. But I wanted a bit more out of him, and gently suggested he might need to give us "a few quid as well..." as Frank mentioned in his Introduction! Two grand later, we did the deal, and somehow, in spite of my hard bargaining, I managed to stay friends with Frank too. And over the years, he became a very useful ally when I stepped up my ambitions. More of that later...

But as one partnership began, another one was ending...

Kenron Racing – the business – was doing well, but Kenron Racing – the partnership – was on its last legs. The going was getting tougher, and the horse and jockey weren't working as a team anymore. Because while Ron was doing all the work, Ken was getting less involved.

The truth is, I was fed up with Ken. He still had his domestic problems, and he had complicated arrangements with his ex and his kids. I certainly knew what that could be like. But we were taking five hundred quid a week wages; I didn't need five hundred quid a week, but Ken wanted to take more and more out of the business all the time. I would have rather used that money to go on developing the business. And that was the biggest problem of all...

A long time ago, we'd talked about our ambitions, but it was clear to me that Ken's ambition had never extended much beyond the here-and-now. So while I was developing a nice little nest egg – a nice little empire for us both – he was hogtied by his commitments.

We were never going to get anywhere together. Our race was run. I told Ken I'd had enough, and I wanted to do my own thing, so we split up, and we split the business. I kept the Upholland shop, and I let him take my old jewel-in-the-crown shop, with a little cash adjustment to make it fair to me. We sold the St Helens shop and Fred Done's old shop.

It was a shame. We'd been flying, but Ken's commitments had been holding back our expansion plans. More than that, we had different dreams. We had different ideas about just how far we could go. In the end, Ken moved to Lancaster, and I think he was happy there. He'd always been a good guy, and we'd had some good laughs along the way, but Ken had always been lazy. He never turned up for security on a Sunday, or ever really pushed himself to look beyond what we already had to what we could have had.

Never mind what I could have had, what I did have was one shop left from four. But Upholland was a good shop, and a good springboard for expanding all over again. I may have lost Ken, but another young man came onto the scene to fill the void. He was a bit raw at first, but I knew he came from good stock! My son, Colin, started work at the Upholland shop in 1985. He'd been in a few times before that, just getting a feel for the place. But like Wally Mills before me, I had to wait until he was eighteen before letting him do anything *officially* in the shop.

We'd had the shop about a year. It was FA Cup Final Day, Manchester United v Everton. A guy we knew very well came into the shop. It was Lenny, a proud Scouser, and at six foot seven, he was a gentle giant of a man – most of the time! If he'd had a bit to drink though, he wasn't quite so lovely.

I was in a little side office and Colin was out on the counter taking the bets. Now, Lenny wanted a tenner on Norman Whiteside to score the first goal in the Cup Final. As it happens, Whiteside did score the first goal. But there was a problem...

The goal was scored well into extra time, at 110 minutes. Unfortunately for him, all football bets were decided at ninety minutes. So if the score was nil–nil on the stroke of ninety minutes, it didn't matter what happened next. It just meant that the bet had been lost. If you had won any money on that result, it would have been on a full-time score of nil–nil.

So having placed his bet, Lenny had gone off to the pub to have a pint or two and watch the game. Then at about six o'clock he turned up, full of booze, thinking he'd won his bet. He slapped the betting slip down on the counter, expecting a nice little payout of £130. And Colin was out front saying, "There's nothing on that, Lenny. Extra time doesn't count."

I could hear the change in Lenny straightaway. Our gentle giant was on the verge of wrecking the place. I went out, grabbed him, and said, "If you don't get out of this shop now, I'm going to throw you out!"

"I want my hundred and thirty pounds!"

"You're getting nothing. Out!"

I was on the verge of hitting him, thinking, *If I don't hit him, he's going to thump me!* But I managed to drag him out of the shop.

Lenny came back in on Monday. He'd sobered up and he was back to his normal self. He couldn't apologise enough. But that was what life was like in a betting shop. Tempers did flare sometimes, but, as long as you had respect for each other underneath it all, things usually worked out alright. Colin hadn't been working in the shop very long, and that was certainly a rude awakening for him. But at least it hadn't been one of the Quality Street Gang! That could have turned out quite differently!

CHAPTER FIVE

TURF WAR

I had very quickly gone from having four shops to having just one. That wasn't the future I had planned out for myself. So when a shop came up for sale on a rough council estate in Leigh in 1986, I went to see a 'rogue' by the name of Bobby Hope. He was skint and agreed to my terms. I poached a manager from a rival, and we got it doing great business. At its height it was making 28% gross profit – that's 6% more than any other shop I'd ever owned.

The shop was packed Monday to Friday, but it was always small sums of money – just the way some bookmakers like it. But then, suddenly, on Saturdays it was empty, and I couldn't get my head around it. It doesn't matter where you are, Saturdays are always your busiest day in a betting shop – but not in Leigh.

I rang Bobby up and asked him what was going on, and he told me that on Saturdays, all the punters went into town, they went to the pubs in the town, and they made their bets in the town-centre betting shops. They had a day out of the estate and away from their wives! We couldn't give them a break from their married lives, and we couldn't even give them a drink because we had no pub!

It was an 'interesting' shop. To say the estate was rough would be an understatement. But it was full of characters – think of the TV series Shameless and you'd be on the right track. I didn't work there much!

Our cashier at Leigh was a hard-as-nails woman called Dawn. She was a great worker, very conscientious and by God, she took no prisoners. She had her quirks though. If she ever dropped any coins on the floor, they'd stay there until around ten minutes before closing time. Then she'd crawl about picking them all up. Heaven knows how her till balanced during the day, but I didn't mind that, she was as good as gold, and the perfect cashier for that shop.

My young protégé Colin was plying his trade, but he hadn't experienced everything that a life in the betting industry could throw at you. So when the manager of the Leigh shop was off sick, I thought it would be an education for Colin...

It was the middle of the day, races were going off every few minutes, and a punter came running up to the counter to place a bet on a race that had just gone off. It was a short distance 'sprint race'. Over the hubbub of the shop, Dawn bellowed back, "I can't take that, you're too late, the race is off."

Predictably, the horse the customer had wanted to bet on won the race. And sure enough, the unhappy punter took to informing all and sundry about his misfortune. Colin was just sitting at the desk, settling bets, when the gentleman loudly said, "Yeah, that fucking cow didn't take my bet."

Like a greyhound out of the trap, Dawn shot out from behind the counter and pinned him to the wall, with her hand around his throat, threatening to perform GBH on him if he didn't retract what he'd said.

A rapid apology followed. Like I said, it was quite the education for young Colin!

By the late Eighties, I was pretty much married to work, and I wasn't getting a break from that relationship any time soon. But it meant there wasn't much time or opportunity for anything else in my life, and my relationship with Maureen crumbled. I bought a house in Winwick, and threw myself back into the business of expanding my portfolio of shops.

But first, I had to deal with the interest I was getting on the Leigh shop. In three short years, I had turned Leigh around, and people had been taking notice. Bookmaking is a pretty simple game if you know what you're doing. The overheads on the Leigh shop were low and I was getting about 25% gross profit. I effectively doubled the turnover that Bobby Hope had been doing. In the end, I got an offer I couldn't refuse, and I sold the shop to Nick Daisley for a nice 80% profit.

We carried on trading at Upholland. It was a consistent earner, and Colin was still learning the ropes, ready to take over when the next stage of the expansion plan kicked in. In 1991, I spotted a couple of promising sites in my home town of Warrington. The first was a shop rental in Westbrook. Going back to Warrington meant that I was back on Fred Done's stomping ground. I guessed that he would have been unhappy with me opening up a new shop on 'his patch'. He already had seven shops there, and, the word was, he felt untouchable. But I was a different proposition to the faceless competition, I was a known quantity, and he knew I was a threat. My suspicions were confirmed when, even before we opened, I had a visit from Fred Done's general manager.

He came straight up to me and said, "Can I have a word with you?"

I knew who it was, and I told him he could have a few words, but not too many, because I was a busy man. He came straight out with it. "Fred's not happy!"

So I said, "That makes me happy. And you can go back and tell him that if you like."

The opening went ahead as planned. I was already well known by punters in the area, so we had a big opening day, and I gave them a good deal. They came from all over Warrington to join in. But a week after we'd opened, another one of Fred's area managers showed up. He walked right into the shop and started doing a head count. He was perfectly brazen about it, he even waved at me when he came in, and gave me a cheery, "Hello, Ron."

He came back the next day, and the next. That third time, I came out from behind the counter, went up to him and said, "You've been in the shop three days on the trot, but you've not had a bet..."

He said, "No I'm just making observations."

So I told him, "I'd rather you didn't."

He seemed put out. "But you know what Fred's like, Ron."

I said, "Yeah, and he knows what I'm like too! So you just let him know that if you come back in this shop tomorrow, I'm going to physically remove you."

He never came back.

That Westbrook shop didn't satisfy me for long, and I had my sights set on another plot too… Off the main road in Fearnhead, there was a massive car park, with a row of council property shops, with flats above them. There was a Chinese takeaway, a newsagent's, a chemist's, and a corner supermarket. There were chimney pots as far as the eye could see, lots and lots of prospective punters, all within easy reach. It was a good catchment area, the best you could get in the early Nineties. Times had changed. The drink-driving laws had been tightened up, not as many people were using the pubs, and the days of the betting shop in a pub car park had gone. This was the next best thing.

There wasn't a betting shop there, and there wasn't a betting shop for more than a quarter of a mile, but there was a piece of land on one edge of the car park that hadn't been built on. So I went to the council and asked them how much they wanted for the land. They wouldn't tell me. They said they had already given provisional planning permission for a day nursery. That didn't discourage me one bit. The land was technically still up for grabs. So I asked them if I could still apply to put a betting shop there, and they said that I could. There could be two or more pending planning permissions. I was willing to pay whatever it took, but of course I didn't tell them that.

I asked, "If I get planning permission for a betting shop, will you sell me the land?"

They said, "No. It'll go up for sealed-bid tenders."

So I made the application, got the planning permission, and at the same time, I applied for a licence for a potential betting shop. A licence doesn't become effective until the shop is built, but I needed it in-hand so that I could start building the shop as soon as I got the site – and I was determined that I was going to get the site! But getting that planning permission gave me a new problem: as soon as you have a planning permission for a betting shop – and a vacant site – it means anyone else can make a bid to put a betting shop on the site. Fred Done, Ladbrokes, William Hill and the rest could all have come sniffing around. And as soon as the council put a notice on the land saying: land for sale by sealed-bid tender, with planning permission granted for a betting shop, I knew it was potentially open season on my prime site.

I was going to have to think one move ahead. I'd noticed that further down the road, there was a pub, and opposite the pub was an avenue into a housing estate. In the estate, there were four shops, and one of them was vacant. And when I saw that, my mind went into overdrive...

I contacted the owner of the shop, and agreed to rent the shop without any intention of ever using it. But getting that licence within a quarter of a mile of my cherry-picked car park gave me some breathing space. At that time, the legislation said that you couldn't have two betting shops within the space of a quarter of a mile. So in theory, people would see my name attached to the vacant shop, with a betting licence application in place, and decide they couldn't take a punt on my preferred car park site.

It sounded good, in theory. But I knew full well that someone could think longer term. Someone with capital to burn and a big existing presence in the area could have bought the car park site, built on it, and called my bluff. Then I would have had to trade in the rented shop on the avenue, or walk away. Anyone looking at it would have seen that it wasn't exactly a prime site, and they would have known that, sooner or later, I would have given up on the shop, letting them swoop into my car park land and made a killing. It was a risk I had to take. And that's when I had a call from none other than Fred Done.

"Ron, I see you've got a licence application for a shop in Fearnhead..."

"That's right, Fred," I said innocently enough.

"Well," he went on. "There's a piece of land just around the corner with planning permission for a betting shop, and it looks full of potential."

He'd obviously been to see it. But he knew that if I got a licence for the rented shop, the pending licence on the car park shop would not be granted. Fred was running scared.

"If you're going to be in the area, then I don't want to be," he said. He already had seven shops in the Warrington area, and he knew this was going to present some serious competition. So he declared himself out of the running. The bluff had worked. But I knew there could well be more of the big boys sniffing around.

I went to get my tender pack and saw that they were numbered. I got number one. That was a good start. There hadn't been any interest before me. I sent Colin along a few days later – just to see what number he'd get. It was number three. Someone we didn't know had been in and got the second pack...

Now it was all a matter of valuing the land. I reckoned it was worth thirty grand, but I knew I'd have to pitch my bid higher to be in with a good chance of winning it. I wanted that land, and when Ron Wadey wants something...

I made a bid of £40,000, and said to myself, *If someone bids more, you'll have to grin and bear it.* I'd done everything I could do.

A few days later the letter arrived. I had won the bid! I still didn't know who had got that second tender pack though. A week later, I was in Culcheth, and I dropped in to see a pal of mine, Peter Rimmer, at his newspaper shop. Peter was a good punter, and he had an account with me. He was one of those punters that thought he could jump over the fence whenever he wanted to, and be a bookmaker. He'd even bought a betting shop on the other side of Leigh.

So I asked him how the betting shop was doing, and he said, "It's doing fine, Ron, but I'm a bit pissed off. I've just missed out; there's a piece of land up for sale in Fearnhead and I put a bid in on it... I didn't get it."

Peter had got pack number two!

He said, "I was the second-highest bidder."

All innocence, I said, "Oh, I know the site you mean, it looks good… So, just as a matter of interest, what was your bid?"

He said, "I bid thirty grand."

I felt sick. I'd have got it for thirty-one!

I left the shop tight-lipped, but Pete found out eventually, and we had a bit of a giggle about it. But I never, ever told him how much I paid for it.

When I'd got over the shock, I was pretty chuffed with myself.

The build was on, and another old pal of mine came into the frame to help me. Dave Hill, the stand-off, the man who used to make me all those tries in my rugby days had become a civil engineer, and he designed the shop for me. He didn't come cheap, but I trusted him and he project managed the entire thing.

The whole project – including the cost of the land at £31,000 (I mean £40,000!) as well as the build, and the shop-fit – cost me a hundred and fifty grand. I'd put some money away from the Leigh sale, but I didn't have that kind of money lying around, so I sold my house. There would be time to settle down later, back then I was more interested in having a portfolio of good shops to my name.

We took 800 bets on our opening day. That was from a standing start. There were established shops in the area that couldn't match that sort of slippage. I ploughed all the money in the Wadey kitty into that shop, and I put on some unbeatable incentives on our opening weekend. The investment really paid off. By then we'd had the Upholland shop for seven years, and the two Warrington shops quickly became good earners. By the mid-Nineties, I was poised to take on more…

Me and everyone else. It was boom time for bookmakers. The big-name shops were expanding their portfolios fast. There were rich pickings for the big boys, but they were cut-throat, and some of the smaller operators were starting to feel the squeeze, and there were people out there who used their buying power to squeeze the little guys out.

There was a shop in Warrington at the end of a row of shops on the main road. There was a good variety of businesses there, and lots of passing trade. It was a great spot for a betting shop and everyone knew it, and coveted it. Someone had their eye on that shop – we'll call him Greg – and he opened up another shop in his empire down a side street off the main road. He traded from it happily enough, but he wanted that shop on the main road. So he went to see the owner, Arthur, and Greg didn't beat around the bush. He told him he'd come to buy the shop – just like I did with Keith Davis – but Arthur wasn't interested. "It's my living," he said. "It's all I've got to feed my family." That was a red rag to a bull as far as our betting-shop magnate was concerned.

The shop itself was a dump: no shop-fit, it was cleaned once a week at best, there were cigarette stubs all over the floor – a disgrace. But Greg knew its real value. He offered Arthur sixty grand for it, and to be fair, that was a good offer, whatever it was turning over. But Arthur was happy with his lot.

Greg went to leave, but as he got to the door, he turned and said, "Fair enough, but don't say I didn't warn you..."

The shop at the other end of the row was a greengrocer's. Greg went to see the owner of that shop too. He bought the greengrocer's, and transferred the licence from the side street to the main road shop.

Now, at that time, bookmakers had to pay betting tax on turnover of around 9% – so we'd charge punters a fee of 10% to cover the cost. If a punter placed a £10 bet, they'd be charged £11, and we'd pay ninety pence of that to Customs and Excise. There was no way you could run a shop tax free and still make it pay. You still had to pay your rent, your staff costs, and your payment to SIS who provided the race coverage.

Greg already had forty shops, and he could afford to make the forty-first shop a loss leader. He went to tax free. He opened up with big notices in the front window advertising tax-free betting. Within one week – just one – Arthur's shop was empty. He didn't have a punter to his name. So he got on the phone...

"Greg, the shop's yours. Sixty grand wasn't it."

"Yeah..." said Greg. "That was last week's price. I'll give you ten grand for it."

Arthur wasn't having it. "No chance," he said and hung up.

Arthur was back within a week. "Greg, give me twenty and you can have the keys." In the end, he walked away with £14,000. And that's how it worked. That story was being repeated all over the country. Even I did it to a woman in Billinge... but I wasn't as ruthless as some of them.

I went to tell her I was opening up a shop down the road. I knew I was going to out-trade her, so I offered her a good price to get out. I reckoned it was worth fifteen to twenty to anyone else; I offered her twenty-five grand, and I promised her I'd keep her niece on – and any of the other staff that wanted to stay.

She had to talk to her husband about it, but I told her, "Call me tomorrow, because I'm going to open in a week, and I will trade you into the ground... But I don't want to do that, so I am making you a very good offer."

She knew it was true. And she was happy to get out.

I could have done what Greg did, but I had my mother's heart – as well as her luck. I wasn't ruthless. Not like him. Not like some of the others.

Her Billinge shop was attached to a pub. Normally, a pub-adjacent betting shop would have given me a good feeling around the wallet area, but times were changing. The old betting shop and pub match didn't always work. In some parts, the old traditions were already changing. The drink-driving laws had certainly changed!

The general area was good though; there was a row of about eight shops, and I had it in the back of my mind to make a move if any of them ever became available. When I saw a For Let sign in one of the windows, I pounced. I closed the shop I'd bought and moved the business a few hundred yards down the road into one of the vacant units.

I didn't need a solicitor, I just used to call Frank. He sorted it all out for me. Frank had started his own consultancy, offering business development services for among others, independent betting shops, and helped me obtain licences, and make all the necessary applications. As Frank tells it, solicitors never liked making licence applications. The requirements for the Betting and Gaming Act were very precise, and the solicitors who didn't understand all the ins and outs of it invariably made mistakes.

Frank got in with Dave Pluck who had seven shops and he did a lot of work marketing the shops very successfully. Dave and Frank built that business up to forty shops and did very well for themselves. I do sometimes wonder what Frank and I could have achieved if we'd put our minds to it. But as it happened, we did achieve a rather interesting coup, which I'll come back to in the next chapter...

So, we added another shop in Rainford. It was another existing business adjoining a pub, but it was a thriving pub; in theory the shop should have been doing good business. But the pub landlord didn't play his part. You'd have expected him to have made the link between better trade in the betting shop leading to better trade in his pub, and vice versa. You would at least have expected him to put the live racing on the TV, so people could nip in and out and place their bets.

I went to see him a few times and told him that if we worked together, we could do good things. But he was just a salaried pub manager, and he wasn't interested. So I went in on Royal Ascot week, when the racing was on, and the TV would be switched off. So he was no help whatsoever. It was a real shame, we could have been taking sixteen or seventeen grand a week – it was a good catchment area – but we only managed about twelve. That was still an increase of about eight grand a week, but compared with Fearnhead, which was doing about thirty-eight thousand a week, it was disappointing. Rainford never really fulfilled its potential, but it was a mark of how far I'd come that I was disappointed by its relative failure. I could tell that the next few years were going to be even more lucrative.

CHAPTER SIX

HEADS I WIN, TAILS YOU LOSE

Never a borrower or a lender be, they say. But in the betting fraternity, they should say, 'Never a bookmaker and a punter be!'

I did 'jump over the fence' once or twice. I became a rugby odds compiler, and was known to make a few shrewd bets on rugby league games. Rugby league was my baby. I knew the teams and I knew their strengths and weaknesses, and the weather was a big factor too. If you can remember it, this was back in the late Eighties, that same week Michael Fish appeared on TV saying he'd been told there was a hurricane coming, but not to worry, there wasn't. Now, the coupons were compiled on the Monday for games being played on the following Saturday, so they couldn't ever factor the weather into the odds at all. And that was the key to it. I had spotted an opportunity in the rugby betting rules that rewarded punters if they correctly identified high-scoring games, and I had been waiting for just the right conditions. This was before they used to water the playing surfaces before the match, or at half time, and the dry, hard conditions invariably led to high-scoring games.

It was time to put my theory to the test! So, as a punter, I put ten separate bets on at ten separate betting shops. I laid out £2,500 in total, at £250 a bet. I put a few of the bets on myself, Colin put some on, and I rang Frank Seymour and told him to put a couple of bets on for me too... and I said he should think very seriously about putting a bet on for himself too.

Some punters will tell you they just knew they were going to win – they could feel it in their water – and some will tell you they were keen students of form. I was in the latter camp. I knew my rugby, and that weekend, I could see which way the results were going to go. It wasn't a premonition, it was just a close study of the form, and a good eye for the way the weather was going to affect the games.

That afternoon, the results started coming in, and the wins (and the winnings) kept on adding up. Every player on every team seemed to have read the script. Hundreds quickly turned into thousands. I passed ten thousand pounds then fifteen, then twenty... Nine results and nine wins later, there was one result still to come. The result was never in any doubt. I had a clean sweep of wins, and a total return of nine times my stake – twenty-five-grand!

Predicting the results – that was the easy part. I knew the difficult bit was going to be collecting the money, but I had no idea just how difficult... I hadn't been given any insider information, and I hadn't set out to target any particular betting shop, but that didn't stop one betting-shop owner from smelling a rat...

Frank had about five grand to collect from two shops, including one of Fred Done's shops. Fred knew who was behind it all, and he would have seen that the same bet had been placed in a number of his shops. So I wasn't surprised when Frank got on the phone saying, "Ron, I've got a problem. They won't pay me."

Fred might have suspected me, but he couldn't prove it, or could he? Frank had paid in cash, and he demanded to be paid in cash. But Fred's manager said he could only pay out by cheque, and he wanted a name to make the cheque out to. My name.

The same thing happened when Colin went around the shops to collect the winnings on the bets he'd placed for me. But we weren't about to let that scare us. I was in no particular hurry for the money, I just wanted to be paid in cash, as was my right as a cash-paying punter! Every month, Frank and Colin went in to ask for their winnings, and every month it was the same. "You can have a cheque." To which the reply was always "No thanks. See you in a month's time." It took about nine months, but, in the end, we got every one of those payments in cash.

Then there was 'the bet of all bets'. It was at the Upholland shop, and I was on my day off. We had a punter who you might best describe as a bit of a lunatic; Gary owned a social club, and didn't seem to have any concerns about money whatsoever. He liked to come into the shop and place some outrageous bets. Now, people said I had balls of steel for the liabilities I'd taken on in the past, but by this time, I had a maximum payout limit; no one could win more than a hundred thousand pounds in any transaction – and that included Gary!

Not many bookmakers would have taken on the bets this guy wanted to place. I'd given him his head before, let him place some sizable bets, but when he ended up owing me money, that was an end to it. That first time, I came to an arrangement with him, and he paid me in central heating! I told him if he couldn't repay his debt, then he'd need to make good on his debt by installing the central heating in one of my shops. He did it gladly. But every time he made a bet with me after that, it was on the strict understanding that I wanted paying in full. My shops were all sufficiently centrally heated by then. His credit days were over.

So that day, he came in with a fifty-pound Canadian bet – that's twenty six-leg bet, at fifty pounds per bet. It all came to a £1,300 investment.

Colin got on the phone...

"Dad..." He drew it out just long enough to let me know something was wrong. "Gary's first two selections have won."

The prices on the two winners were 7/2, and 9/2. So, I told Colin to tot up Gary's likely winnings, based on the prices of the next three horses. We were looking at the tidy sum of a hundred grand. It was turning into the worst day out I'd ever had!

All was not yet lost. We had accounts with Hills, Ladbrokes and Corals, but my maximum credit was £500 at each. I knew we'd need a £1,500 treble on the last three horses to cover the liability. I had some cash in my pocket, so I went to Sankey Street in Warrington, where there was a William Hill's and a Coral's. My mate Dave was now the manager of the Coral shop. So I told him I was in trouble, and needed to put on a big bet.

"I want fifteen hundred to be honest, but will you take a thousand-pound treble?"

Dave thought for a moment and said he'd take it.

"The full thousand?"

"Nah," he said. "Give me the fifteen hundred."

He rang it through to head office, and I paid in cash.

I can remember the third horse – it was called Access Travel, and I can remember it because it was the only odds-on horse in Gary's bet. At 4/6, it was a virtual certainty.

It lost.

But we were still in trouble. If the remaining two horses won, we'd still have a liability of thirty-three thousand, at least. The market was fluctuating, we didn't know what the starting prices were going to be, so we needed a little wiggle room. So I upped the ante. "Better make it thirty-six thousand,"

That meant a £1,500 double. So I told Colin to put on a £500 double at William Hill's, another at Ladbrokes, and another with Coral.

Both horses won, and I had to pay Gary his £33,000. But later, we received three cheques off Ladbrokes, William Hill and Coral for the combined total of £36,000. We were £3,000 up. And Gary's £33,000? He lost it all to me in the next six months.

So, I won on the rugby, I won on the horses, and I won on the dogs too...

I was always interested in diversifying my portfolio of interests, and dogs was the natural next step. I bought some greyhounds and got them trained for me in Ireland. The trainer was giving me good feedback on a dog of mine called Lipton, so I went over to Dublin to watch her first race with a couple of pals.

Lipton won her race at 5/2, and inspired by our success we went for a drink. My friend Paul was a very heavy drinker – he could down ten pints as easily as you like – and as the drinks went down, he would get louder and louder. The British Open was on at the time, and my other friend John had placed a bet at the shop of £1,000 at 7/2 on the Frenchman, Jean van de Velde to win. At the end of the third day, we came back from the dog racing to see that van de

Velde already had a commanding lead going into the last day. So the two of them were laying into me that night saying I was going to have to pay up the next day.

With Lipton's race run, we'd decided to stay in Dublin, get a pub lunch, and watch the golf through to the finish. After the high of my victory the night before, the Sunday was getting worse and worse. Van de Velde was three shots clear coming into the last two holes, and it meant I was looking at a payout of three and a half thousand quid. I didn't mind losing, and I'd certainly had my share of big payouts over the years, but the one thing I couldn't take was Paul getting more and more drunk and rubbing salt in the wound!

"It's going to be an expensive weekend for you, Wadey!" he said, getting louder and more in-my-face with each pint.

Six pints in myself, I'd had more than enough, and by the time the players approached the eighteenth tee, I ventured, "You know what you two can do," and stormed off back to the hotel and went straight to bed. I didn't even turn on the TV, I didn't want to see the last rites being carried out!

I was up early for my flight the next morning. Out of habit, I went across the road to buy the *Racing Post*, and there was a big picture of the Open winner on the back page... Paul Lawrie! *Is this last year's paper?!* I couldn't believe it. It turns out that van de Velde had driven into the water on the eighteenth hole. Then there'd been a play-off, and he'd just lost it. All that composure that had taken him so far, gone. Bad luck for him. My mother's luck for me.

I couldn't wait to see Paul and John emerge, bleary-eyed, into a very bright Dublin morning! They didn't half get some stick.

CHAPTER SEVEN

THE ODD COUPLE

With five shops in the portfolio, I needed people I could trust working for me, and I wanted someone I wouldn't ever have any doubts in employing looking after the Westbrook shop. I knew there was someone who was still living and working in Warrington who would fit the bill...

My old pal, David Moore, had stayed working at Mark Lane's in Manchester after they'd been taken over by Coral. David was the guy I'd worked with at Mark Lane's back in my twenties, and he was the guy who had let me make a bet to cover the liability on the Canadian bet. I knew he had all the qualities I wanted in a manager. Most of all, he got on well with the punters; I knew I could rely on him to run a profitable shop. He jumped at the chance to manage the Westbrook shop, while Colin went to run Fearnhead.

It was funny how our lives came back together at that time. David had just split up from his wife, so as well as giving him a job, I suggested he come and share the cost of a house with me. It made a lot of sense; as well as halving our costs, it meant I could drop him off at the Westbrook shop every morning. Having passed his driving test, David had never actually driven a car in his life.

Twenty-three years after we'd met, we took out a twelve-month lease on a house and lived an odd-couple lifestyle for the best part of a year. The house was just a standard two-up, two-down. I had the front bedroom, and he had the back bedroom. The bathroom was at the top of the stairs. So whenever I went to the bathroom, I had to walk past his bedroom on my left. I was up early one morning, ready to leave the house at eight o'clock. While I was getting dressed, I heard David getting up and going to the bathroom. I heard him very clearly because he didn't close the bathroom door – I think he thought I'd already left for work, and he must have assumed he had the whole house to himself. So as I left my room to go down the stairs, he opened the bathroom door and I got a full-frontal. He panicked, flew into his bedroom and slammed the door shut. As I walked past, I said, "Well, I've seen everything now!"

David was quite a character, and we had many laughs together. There was one incident that really sticks in my mind – and when you've read about it – it's probably going to stick in yours too. Sorry about that!

Now, David was a big drinker, and when he got settled in for a proper session, he'd be at the bar all day. Sunday was his big drinking day. The betting shops were still closed on a Sunday in those days, so he could really let his hair down. He went out at twelve o'clock sharp, and got himself bedded in for an eight-hour session. He always went to the same pub, and in the evening he always came back with his son, Ashley, who would have been about nine years old at the time. The boy's mother would drop by the pub, pick up the ever-so-slightly inebriated David and drop them both off back at our two-up, two-down.

On one particularly hot summer afternoon, I was doing my usual Sunday security work, and by four o'clock, I'd had more than enough. So I downed tools and, although I never normally drank in the day, I wanted a pint. So I went to David's pub. By that time, he'd have downed about six pints of bitter, and was just moving into top gear. He was in his usual position, leaning against a pillar, facing the bar. He took up that same spot, week in, week out.

I asked him if he was ready for a pint, knowing full well what the answer would be. David would never say no if a pint was offered to him, even if he had three quarters of a pint on the go. We drank our pints, and David bought another round. By half past five I was ready for something to eat and I left him there to get a few more pints in!

He came back at eight o'clock as usual, and I heard him struggling to get the key in the door. He was properly drunk, there was no doubt about it. He had a big bag of Chinese takeaway for them both. I was working quietly in the living room, when David blundered in with Ashley, crashed their meal down on the table and turned the TV on.

I wasn't having that, I still had a lot of work to do, and I didn't want that kind of distraction. So I told him the best thing he could do was eat up, then get to bed, and sleep the beer off. He got the hump with me then. So he turned the TV off, and they ate their meals in silence. Then, like a scalded cat, he stropped off upstairs. I heard him making his slow way up the stairs and went out to the hall, just to make sure he was alright. He was about two thirds of the way up, when he slipped.

Now David was a big chap – probably about seventeen stones in weight – and when he slipped, he fell face down and lay there like a beached whale. He was hanging on to one of the steps, three from the top. We were in hysterics at the bottom of the stairs. The poor chap didn't know what to do – he didn't know whether he should try to stand up, and risk falling backwards, or whether he should just let go and let gravity take its toll. Eventually, he let go and came down, step by ignominious step on his stomach. His chin hit each and every step on the way down. It was one of the most hilarious things I'd seen in my life, and we were in pieces.

By the time he'd chinned his last step, we had a seventeen-stone man at the bottom of the staircase, and somehow we had to get him back up the stairs, and pack him off to bed. Somehow, we got him on his feet, and I (bravely or stupidly?) said, "I'll be right behind you, so if you fall, I'll do what I can to keep hold of you!" We managed to get him to the top, and he crawled off to bed after that.

I think we were both happy to move out on our own again after the full-frontal and the staircase incident, but David carried on looking after the shop, and we stayed the best of friends. On Boxing Day 1998, David was working with me at the Upholland shop which had always been – and would remain – our head office. It had been a good day – Boxing Day always was – and I was carrying two identical holdalls as we locked up and left the shop. In one of them, I had a thousand pounds worth of pound coins, just in case one of the shops needed some at short notice. In the other, I had the day's profits of about £3,000. Every one of our shops always had a safe – all except Upholland, so I used to drop off the profits at our Billinge shop, on my way home, so I could bank it the next working day.

My car was parked right outside the door of the shop in a little recess, and there was a side street opposite across the main road. David was going around to the passenger side, while I was opening up the boot to put the bags in. And that's when David shouted, "Ron, mugger!"

I looked up to see a tall bloke in a balaclava, brandishing a twelve-inch knife, standing right next to me. I'd just put the bags in the boot, and in that split second I knew that if I could close the boot and get into the next-door supermarket, he'd probably run off. Adrenalin coursing through me, I slammed the boot down so hard that it shot straight back up again, exposing both the bags.

I told him to put the knife down; I said we could sort it out, but he kept shouting that he wanted my money.

I tried to put him off. I said, "I haven't got any money in my pockets."

He said, "It's in the boot, isn't it?"

He put his head in the boot, grabbed one of the bags and ran across the road and back down the side street he'd come out of. I reached into the boot and lifted the remaining bag. Which one had he taken? The bag with the notes and coins in it was the one in my hand. He'd had a fifty-fifty choice and he taken the lighter bag; the wrong bag.

My mother's luck was shining down on me again. We knew we wouldn't be able to catch him, so we drove back to the Billinge shop, and cool as a cucumber, I rang the police. But afterwards, when I got back in the car to drive home, I started to shake, and my life flashed in front of my eyes. That night in bed, all I could see when I closed my eyes was the knife.

I went into the police station the next day to give them as much of a description as I could, but they never caught him. He got cheque books and accounts books, nothing of any value. I'd put that down as another good result for Ron Wadey.

***

David repaid all of my trust in him. He never did re-marry. Neither did I. And I think it's just as well for everyone that we didn't. While I stayed married to the business, David was always going to be a tough prospect for a wife. I'd lived with him for a year, and that had been enough for me! And then there was his lifestyle...

It wasn't that David was an alcoholic, he just had a big thirst! And he was never happier than when he had a pint in his hand. But the lifestyle caught up with him in the end. He was only in his sixties when he ended up in hospital. He went there to die.

We all knew he was destined to drink himself to death. The death certificate said: Cirrhosis of the liver. Just like George Best.

I was with him a couple of hours before he died. The last thing I did was try to spoon feed him a yoghurt, but he was already slipping away. Ashley arrived. He was in his twenties then. He asked me if I would be going back later, but I shook my head sadly. I knew he was going to die in the next twenty-four hours. I told Ashley that I'd said my goodbyes to his dad. I got home at around midday. Just after three o'clock, the phone rang. It was Ashley; his dad had died.

I paid for David's funeral. He was on his own, he was divorced, and I didn't want Ashley to have to pay. His family asked me to do his eulogy, and I did most of it. But I broke down before I could finish.

He was a good mate – one of the best – and a very funny man. He was one of those people who didn't know just how funny he was! He didn't try to be funny; he just had the knack for making you crack up.

I had a lot to thank him for – he turned me into a Manchester City supporter for one! And we had a lot of laughs together over the years.

Cheers, mate.

CHAPTER EIGHT

THREE HEART ATTACKS!

I first got my son Colin into the shop back in the Labour Club days, our old jewel in the crown. He'd been about fourteen then. He had shown an aptitude for maths – not as keen an aptitude as mine though – and he was keen to learn the ropes. It was only ever on Saturdays, and I hid him away around the corner, out of sight. I could see he had the same passion for it – my dad had passed it down another generation – so I had given him a few bets to work out. He didn't get paid!

By the time he was eighteen, I got him in at Upholland. And then I started to pay him a wage! Colin took to the territory quickly, and we've been working together ever since. In fact, we've been working together so long now that I've said he'll have to do my eulogy! It hasn't been like a normal father / son relationship; more like best mates. People can't believe the way we speak to each other sometimes! And there have been a few rows along the way. After one particularly bad argument, Colin went AWOL for a whole week! I can't even remember what we'd been arguing about now, but I got him on the phone and gave him an ultimatum: "It's all water under the bridge now. Stop your sulking. Get into work tomorrow, or fuck off forever!"

He was in bright and early the next morning.

Our working relationship carried on more-or-less smoothly after that, but there was one time when he nearly gave me a heart attack. It all started when I was rushed into hospital with a suspected heart attack – although I couldn't pin that one on Colin...

I'd been playing badminton. My opponent was twenty-five; I was forty. He was six foot four; I'm five foot ten. He was thin as a rake; I had a bit of a beer belly. There was only ever going to be one winner! I ran him close a few times though. He beat me 15–12 in the first set. I had enough fire left in my belly for the second set, so I psyched myself up for it and gave it my all. He still beat me 15–13.

We had a soft drink afterwards, and I was absolutely knackered. I'd given everything I had, and he noticed something was wrong because, unusually for me, I never said a word. I felt more drained than I had ever felt in my life.

He looked worried and said, "Something's wrong, isn't it."

Through gritted teeth I said, "I think I'm having a heart attack..."

He dialled 999, and the ambulance came and took me to Macclesfield Hospital. They kept me in overnight, did a few tests, and when the consultant came in to see me the next day, he wanted to ask me a few questions.

"Do you smoke, Mr Wadey?"

I told him, "Unfortunately, yes."

"How many do you smoke?"

"I buy twenty a day but I don't smoke twenty a day," I told him. "Because of the job I do, I light a cigarette, and then I don't smoke it. I stick it in the ashtray and it burns out because I'm busy."

It was true. I only really smoked when I had a few pints after work, and I certainly never smoked in the morning. That didn't stop me coughing up some horrible stuff in the mornings, and I wanted to stop.

He carried on. "My medical advice to you is that you should stop, because there's a slight shadow on one of your lungs."

He said he wasn't too concerned about it – it was just a very slight shadow – but it needed to be monitored. I had some cigarettes in my pocket, and I asked the nurse to hand them to me. She said, "You can't smoke in here..."

"I'm not going to smoke them," I said, and screwed them up. I handed her the remains and asked her to put them in the bin. As a bookmaker, I'd say it was evens on that the doctor was bluffing. He was trying to scare me into stopping, but it worked. I've never had a cigarette since.

They kept me in anyway, and did some more tests, and then on the third day, I got a call from Colin in the Upholland shop. He was about twenty-one at the time, and he was shitting bricks. Nervously he told me, "I've got a Yankee bet here, and the first two have won..."

Very calmly, I asked him to estimate how much it was going to cost us if the next two horses won. I talked him through it all very carefully. "When you've worked it out, you'll need to have a double with another bookmaker on the last two, to cover the liability."

By this point, I was already out of bed and halfway through the door. I signed myself out of hospital and got in a taxi back to the shop. The old grey cells leaped into action and I was working out the liability on the way. I calculated that the most he'd need was a hundred-pound double. If they were two 5/1 chances, it would work out at £3,600 for a hundred-pound double – maybe eighty quid would be enough – and that would cover us. I wouldn't have let anyone win £3,600 for a £55 bet, it would have taken me forever to rake that back. So I resolved it wouldn't be my money they were going to get, it'd be William Hill's money!

In the end, it worked out that a sixty-pound double would have done it. So I was racing back, knowing the third race would have been run by the time I got back to the shop. Breathless, I burst through the door, saying, "How did those horses get on?"

"They lost," Colin said. "But it's okay, I covered it anyway."

I waited...

He said, "I had a six-hundred-pound double!"

And that's when I nearly had a heart attack for real.

"Six hundred pounds?! Just go over your figures again will you, Colin?"

Realisation struck. "I put the decimal point in the wrong place!" I could hear the pain in his voice as he realised his mistake. But I was very forgiving. I knew he wouldn't make that mistake again, and I never brought the subject up again after that. Well, almost never!

***

Our Fearnhead shop ended up doing eighteen hundred bets every Saturday at an average of fifteen quid a bet. As long as you're not using Colin's maths, that means you take over twenty-five grand on a Saturday.

I'd gone from owning a little shop next to a pub that did a couple of hundred quid profit a week to making five grand profit a week. I'd done it right. But it seems that word had got around that business was booming…

After I'd moved out of the rented accommodation, I bought myself a nice house and a dog called Hudson, named after the butler in *Upstairs Downstairs*, and I'm very glad that I did. It was eight o'clock at night when the doorbell rang. I wasn't expecting anyone, but I got up and went to the door, and Hudson came with me. I could see the frame of a large man in the porch. It wasn't somebody I recognised. I opened the door, and he lunged straight at me.

I managed to hold him off just enough so I could hit him, and I landed a fine right hook which sent him sprawling onto his backside. I wasn't a fighter by any means, but I gave him a good right hook that any boxer would be proud of. And then the back-up leaped into action. I said one word to Hudson: "Kill," and that's all it took.

Hudson was on him in an instant, and that's when I saw the second bloke, who'd been hiding out of the way, turn tail and run off down the drive.

The guy was shouting, "Get him off, get the bastard off me."

But I wasn't having it. "No way, mate. He's having his dinner!"

I knew I would have been beaten up pretty badly – or much worse – if it hadn't been for Hudson, and I gave him a good few minutes at his 'dinner'. By the time I pulled the dog away, there was blood everywhere.

The bloke legged it then, and I'll bet he never tried the same tactic with anyone else. The police didn't need to hear about it, they might have had Hudson put to sleep if they'd come round and seen the blood!

***

As the Eighties wore into the Nineties, we had five shops on the books, and the potential for more, so we set up a limited company, Ron Wadey Bookmakers Ltd. Our audited accounts from 1995 to 1998 showed pre-tax profits of a quarter of a million a year, after expenses. They were good days. Everything went in the expansion pot. I still had a vision. I could see opportunities and knew how to make the most of them.

I knew I had the potential to be a millionaire. That wasn't pride on my part, and it wasn't avarice. It was just mathematics. If the shops carried on performing as well as they had, it would just happen; it was inevitable. But with five shops in the portfolio, I was working harder, and working longer hours than ever before. I was working myself to a standstill, and something was going to give if I didn't cut back. But how could I?

On the one hand, I knew that I would never have it this good again, but on the other I was aware that I was potentially working myself into an early grave. I had already seen too many of the people I had grown up with die much too young. But even when I was working myself to the bone, I still loved the business. The passion for it was still there. (It still is, even today.)

Sunday betting had started, and I got in ahead of the game on that. Before the shops opened on Sundays in Britain, the racetracks in Ireland were all doing good business on a Sunday. So I decided to open up my shop to show the racing from Ireland on Sundays. Nobody else was doing that. The big boys didn't want to bring the staff in on double-time to look after it, so we were the only ones, we were the instigators of betting shops opening on a Sunday. We gave the industry its proof of concept.

By 1993, we were allowed to open for night racing too. Before that, we'd had to close the shop – by law – no later than half past six. It was just about late enough for dog racing, but nothing else.

You could still take a bet on a night race, but you had to take the bets home and get the results off Teletext! The night racing season started in May and didn't finish until August. So for those five months, I was working ninety-hour weeks. I was leaving the house at 8.00 a.m., and getting home at 11.00 p.m., six days a week. By the end of every August, I was a zombie! But help was at hand.

In the mid-Nineties we had a girl working for us who also used to do a night shift in her other job. Having already worked a seven-hour shift, and grabbed a couple of hours' sleep, she came into her job as a cashier at the betting shop. She was a good worker and we got on well. She could see how tired I'd been getting and one day she said, "Psst, Ron, you should take one of these..."

She handed me some Pro Plus. "It's just caffeine," she said. "You buy it over the counter at the chemist. It'll give you a bit of a boost."

So I dosed myself up and felt a bit better for a few hours. Problem solved. The next summer, as the days lengthened and the night racing ran on longer into the evenings, I remembered the Pro Plus, and went back to the chemist to stock up for another summer of ninety-hour weeks. It was all fine, it just meant that at the end of every August, I was absolutely hooked on caffeine! By the time we got down to our last shop – Fearnhead – I was only working two days a week, and Colin was working the other five. And with five days off and time to rest, I had transformed myself into a nine-hours-of-sleep-a-night man!

I was manning the shop on one of Colin's days off, and I was suffering. I'd had a rare night out the night before and got well and truly drunk. I hadn't got home until two in the morning, and I knew I had to be in the shop before nine o'clock. Never mind nine hours a night, I went to work that day on six hours' sleep, head pounding. I felt like death warmed up. But it was alright, I had my secret weapon. I knew a blast of Pro Plus would perk me right up.

I'd kept some in the kitchen at work, and after an hour and a half, I needed them. I was still half-drunk, and I could hardly stand up. I took two Pro Plus and waited for them to kick in. By half past eleven, I felt so bad that I had to ask one of the customers to come behind the counter and take some bets!

I was getting more and more ill. So I took another couple of Pro Plus, rang Colin, and said he'd have to come in. When he arrived, he took one look at me and said, "You're as white as a ghost, what's wrong?" I was never ill. I don't think anybody had known me take a day off in my working life. I told him I'd had a heavy night, and I'd had some Pro Plus. I thought it'd be alright in twenty minutes, but it wasn't.

I went and sat down in the office, and that's when the palpitations started! I said to Colin, "You'd better ring 999, I think I'm having a heart attack!"

The paramedics came and helped me out of the shop. I refused the stretcher – there were people in the shop, and I didn't want rumours going round Warrington that I'd had a heart attack. They gave me an ECG, and they said I definitely hadn't had a heart attack – but I needed to go in and have some tests.

The truth was, I'd been having palpitations for twenty-odd years. I just hadn't told anyone about them before. But I fell in love with the young doctor at hospital and told her everything! She asked me what I'd been up to, and I told her I'd been out, had a bit much to drink, and gone into work, bolstered by some Pro Plus.

She asked me if I still had the Pro Plus; she wanted to check the expiry date. So I rang Colin and asked him to check. They were six months out of date, and the doctor said, "Well, Mr Wadey, that explains it. Pro Plus ferments! If you've taken four of them, that would probably equate to a low dose of heroin!"

While I was reeling from that and coming off my heroin-style-trip, she hit me with another blast of cold reality.

"And those palpitations you've been having... do you drink a lot of coffee?"

I told her I drank loads of coffee.

"Then it sounds to me as if you've got an allergy to caffeine. I think you should switch to decaffeinated coffee from now on."

So I did. I ditched the coffee, and I have never had a single palpitation since. But after two suspected heart attacks, and Colin nearly giving me a third, I knew I had to start taking things a little bit easier.

My parents – Kathleen and Len – on their wedding day.

My christening at St John's Church, Earlestown.

Jockey potential.

District Church of England School, Earlestown. (Spot the young Ron Wadey, and the future Lancs County Cricket club captain, David Hughes, answers at the back of the book.)

Nine years old in Bank Street, Earlestown (note the cobbled street).

The now-extinct Bookmaker's Rule Book and Ready Reckoner, circa 1977.

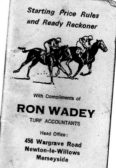

On a rare night out with Mum.

Lipton, winner of the Irish Cesarewitch Consolation race.

Presenting the trophy to the winner of The Ron Wadey sponsored race at Neil Fairbrother's testimonial evening at Belle Vue.

Winter Fair at Kilkenny. (Gamble landed at 9/4 into 'no offers').

Winter Fair does it again. (Another gamble landed 10/1 into 4/1).

Arepeadoubleyou, Tote Gold Trophy winner. Left to right, Francie Murray (trainer), Joe Walsh (Irish government minister), me, and Patricia Griffin (sponsor).

Metric Flower, Irish Oaks runner-up 1999, with trainer, Pat Gaffney.

Catherine and Francis Murray with Arepeadoubleyou, Tote Gold Trophy winner, 2000.

Cartmel, in the tented village (after work, of course)!

With my daughter, Michelle, at Uttoxeter.

With Tony at Chester Races.

With Cartmel MD, Jonathan Garrett.

Looking dapper at Royal Ascot.

Derby Day at Epsom.

With some admirers at Uttoxeter Ladies' Day.

With David and Colin at Cartmel.

With Tony and Colin in Galway.

Working at Listowel.

The one and only Peter McGrane with Sendinpost.

The late Freddie Wray, Newmarket farrier for Geoff Wragg and Henry Cecil.

In Portugal (with unnamed companion).

Tennis drills at Stockton Heath Tennis Club.

My tennis partner, Seb Taylor, in 2018 (at 13 years old).

With Michelle.

Bookie on a bike.

Dessie at 3 months old.

CHAPTER NINE

GONE TO THE DOGS

Through the latter part of the Nineties, our audited figures showed a quarter of a million quid a year profit from our five betting shops. Not bad for somebody who started with five hundred quid! It felt like a real rags-to-riches story, but I knew it couldn't last forever.

By the late Nineties, the industry was changing fast. The old restriction on how many betting shops you could have in an area were lifted. In my day you couldn't have two betting shops within a quarter of a mile proximity. That meant you had your own territory and nobody else could step on your toes. But then, just as I was selling up, that all changed, and suddenly you could have a Betfred next to a Ladbrokes next to a William Hill, all within a hundred yards of each other. Shops were springing up on high streets and in town centres in large numbers – all occupying a small patch of territory, and all vying for the same customers.

It wouldn't have been sustainable, but for the fact the roulette machines came in. They were a huge success, but you were restricted to four per shop. So if your punter couldn't get on a machine in Betfred they'd nip next door to William Hill. But when the maximum spin came down from £100 to £2, it killed it. Those machines had been keeping the betting shops alive. In the end, they killed the goose that laid the golden egg.

The shops are in an even worse state now. After they peaked in value in 2004, the long, slow decline began. At the time of writing, the prospects for the shops that remain are even worse. Online betting was still in its infancy in the mid-2000s, but it's made the whole process of betting so easy. If I know one thing, it's that punters are essentially lazy, and once they've tried online betting, they won't go back to the shops. Why should they? The atmosphere and the camaraderie that used to make the shops so special has all gone.

We were better off out of it, and I knew I didn't want Colin to feel forced into living the life I'd led. I had turned myself into a workaholic for seven or eight years, and I'd sacrificed an awful lot in pursuit of my ambition. I had compromised my relationship with Michelle's mother. We had never married, partly because I had already been married to the business. I knew full well that if I had ever had to choose between them, there would only ever have been one winner.

There was still money to be made in bookmaking, but the industry was much less about individuals. It was all a lot more corporate, and I was starting to feel like it was time to get out, time to downsize the portfolio, while the going was still good.

Over the years, I'd refined the portfolio and whittled it down to five key shops. I sold four of them to Dave Pluck in 1999 – the company that Frank Seymour had gone to be managing director of. At one time, Dave Pluck's estate of forty betting shops was valued at £35 million, including the freeholds they'd purchased. Today? Excluding the freeholds, that business won't be worth £4 million. The bottom dropped right out of the market. But I couldn't help wondering what would have happened if Frank had come to work with me instead. We could have been a great combination.

By 2002, I was fifty-five, and after twenty years of working more hours every year, I was ready for a holiday! By the time we sold Fearnhead to Ladbrokes, the turnover was around thirty-eight grand a week. We sold the business for £750,000, but retained the property, and carried on taking in rent. In the seventeen years since then, I've had over two hundred grand in rent. Not a bad investment all in all! Ladbrokes closed the Fearnhead shop in 2020; it just wasn't viable. A shop like that doesn't exist anymore.

I got out at the right time though, or almost the right time. The Fearnhead sale went through in 2003. If I'd waited one more year, I'd have got the optimal return on my investment. But if I'd left it two years, I'd have made far less; the industry was beginning to implode. So on balance, I was very happy with the way it turned out. I made my six-figure sum, and I was satisfied with what I'd achieved.

Bookmakers are all greedy. I'm the only one I know that isn't greedy! The money was certainly nice, but I'd always been too busy to spend it anyway, or investing it back into expanding the portfolio. The money was never what motivated me. I'd been far more interested in making sure I made the most of the opportunities that came my way.

So when it came to an end, I didn't feel any great sadness, or feel like I was turning my back on the empire I'd been building, I felt as if I'd achieved what I'd been capable of achieving. And I did wonder whether racing was going to let me go quite so easily.

With the last shop sold, I finally decided it was time for a holiday. I went to Portugal, and completely fell in love with the Algarve. I started playing tennis, a lot of tennis. Sport had always been the cornerstone of my young life, but I'd been practically sedentary for three decades. I had an eye for tennis though, my instincts were still pretty sharp, and like everything else that had ever been worthwhile in my life, I threw myself into it one hundred per cent.

I think I would have been a very good player if I'd taken it up as a teenager. I've certainly got all the shots. My playing proficiency probably peaked three years ago. I was playing with two replacement knees then! One of them was eight years old, and the other one was six years old. But I was determined to go on playing to a better standard, and I didn't want the pain in my knees to stop me.

I went all over the world to watch tennis too. Over the next few years there were three trips to the Australian Open, three trips to the US Open, and numerous trips to Wimbledon. I saw tournaments in Switzerland, Germany, China, Canada and France. I was devoted to it.

But reality hit home quickly. After a few months off, I was ready to get back to work. At fifty-six years of age, I still had a lot to give.

There was no point going back to the old empire-building days; the golden age of the betting shop had passed, but I still couldn't quite leave the old life behind.

I'd already taken an interest in dog racing, and put the word out to my friends in Ireland that I'd be interested in looking at any more opportunities to invest. My friend Pat Gaffney rang me up and said he'd seen a bitch called Metric Flower, bred by Larry Byrne, running in a novice stakes. He said she'd been knocked over at the first bend, and still went on to finish third. He reckoned that if she'd stayed on her feet, she'd have won by twenty lengths. It meant there was no good form on her card, but what's on the card doesn't always tell you what happened in the race. So Pat said he was going to buy her and train her. They wanted three grand, he said, and it was a pinch at the price. Even if Pat had inflated the price he'd quoted me to squeeze a little extra out for himself, it would have been worth a punt.

In her first race for us, we fed her up before she ran and, surprise surprise, she ran a lethargic race. Now her card read one third place, and one last. That wasn't going to inflate her starting price. But two weeks later when she ran again, she went into the traps hungry for her dinner, and ready to tear that hare in two!

Pat asked me how much I was going to put on and I switched the question round. "How much would you have on her, Pat?"

Pat said, "I want you to put a thousand quid on for me, and that's just for starters."

"But you haven't got a thousand quid, Pat!"

He said, "I'll train the dog for nothing if I have to, but it won't come to that. There is no danger; this dog is going to win."

That was good enough for me. I added on four thousand. The next problem was finding someone who'd be willing to take the bet. Pat reckoned there was only one man in Ireland willing to take us on – a mate of his called Ted. Ted only ever took on bets from people he knew that he wouldn't normally win any money off. Why? Because we knew that as soon as we put our five thousand on, Ted would probably make a little investment of his own. And so long as our bet went on first – before a flurry of bets brought the odds down – that was fine with us. Another mate of ours, Larry Dunne, made the bet for us, and in the end, we managed to get ten grand on at 3/1.

The race wasn't even close. She won by ten lengths.

Pat gave her a good rub down, a long drink and a meal, and she settled down in the back of his van, while we went to meet Larry in the pub. Larry handed over our twenty grand, the fifteen that I'd won and my original stake. After I downed eight pints of Guinness, I made my way back to my B&B and collapsed on the bed.

In the morning, I couldn't believe what I was seeing. There was money all over the bed and the bedroom floor. There was money everywhere. I must have gone in, taken fistfuls of money out of my brown paper bag and – WHOOO! – thrown it all over the place. It wasn't the money that did it for me – I'd had that much money and more in my hands before – it was the thrill of the moment. It was another coup, like taking all that money off Fred on the rugby bet.

Metric Flower was such a good bitch, and she went on to have forty-nine puppies, over seven litters. They went for £2,000 a piece, which I split with the trainer. Only one of them was any good on the track though, a dog called Double Take, which won the TV Trophy by a diminishing length. He just held on to win, but he never won another race after that.

After that, I'd sit up and take notice any time Pat had another dog to recommend. So when he called to tell me about a dog called Winter Fair, bred by Joe Graham, I was all ears. And when I went to see him run, I liked what I saw. He was a sleek, glossy, brindle dog – the same sort of dark chocolatey colour as my Bull Mastiff, Dessie (named after Desert Orchid, of course).

A chap called Chris Lund trained Winter Fair for me, and gave the dog a solo trial around Belle Vue to give him some track knowledge. Setting off from Trap Three, he did an average time. I told Chris to seed him wide, so that he'd get Traps Five or Six. I was half-right. Put him in Traps One to Five, and he was nothing special, but put him in Trap Six and he was a different dog! I wouldn't ever have backed him out of Trap Five, but he never lost a race form Trap Six. He wanted to be right on top of the hare.

He wasn't much fancied in his first race at Belle Vue. He had odds of 10/1. But anyone that knew me or Chris sat up and took notice when they heard we were involved, and then the bets started piling in. His odds kept dropping, and by the time Colin got involved, he was already down to 4/1!

The traps opened and... Boom! He was gone. Five lengths clear at the first bend. He tired towards the end but still won by two lengths. As he rounded that last bend, the commentator was calling him "the gamble of the year!" But little did he know; out of Trap Six, the result was never in doubt.

Now, whenever a 33/1 shot wins a race, it means the bookmaker is pretty much guaranteed a clear book and one hundred per cent profit, the bookmakers shout "Aye-Aye!" You do it to wind the punters up, obviously. They hate it, they hate bookmakers really! But we all shared in the "Aye- Aye's!" that night. He won another big race in Kilkenny out of Trap Six, and I won four and a half grand out of him that night at 9/4. As soon as he was put in Trap Six, you knew you were onto a sure thing.

I also had a dog in the Tote Gold Cup at Shelbourne Park in Dublin, with a £10,000 prize for the winner. My dog was a big black-and-white dog, trained by Francis Murray, and I called him Arepeadoubleyou (get it?). People used to say, "How do you pronounce that?" And I had to tell them, "It's my initials – RPW!" He was a fearsome dog. You certainly didn't stroke him. I put my hand out to stroke him in the kennel once and nearly ended up with a couple of fingers missing.

I might have forgiven him for nipping a finger off if he won the Tote Gold Cup, of course. And sure enough, he did win it. And I left that day with a ten grand first prize, and all my fingers intact.

CHAPTER TEN

THIS SPORTING LIFE

I'd had a holiday and I had a great time travelling the world. The dogs had helped ease the transition from life in the bookmaking shops to life outside, but after thirty years of working non-stop, something was definitely missing from my life. I told Colin, "I've got to get back to work! I'm bored out of my head. I can't do anything else. I'm a bookmaker."

If I wasn't going to be a bookmaker in a betting shop, then I was going to get out to the racetracks. We'd bought a couple of pitches – just as an experiment a few years earlier, to see if we liked it. But that's when we started buying up pitches in earnest.

We bought a pitch at Cheltenham after I did the deal with Ladbrokes in the March, just in time for the Cheltenham Festival. The timing was (almost) perfect. But when we got to Cheltenham on the Tuesday, I looked at my phone and saw that I had about six missed calls. It was my son David. He said, "Dad, it's your mum. She's had a massive heart attack. She's in a coma in intensive care."

Mother was already in the hospital; she had colon cancer. It was untreatable. She had been given palliative care in hospital since January, but we knew there was nothing more they could do for her. I had always been very close to my mum, and I think I carried a little weight of guilt that I hadn't given her quite as much time as she had deserved. But, I thought ruefully, *I hadn't been able to give anybody the time they deserved, and that includes me*. I had just been so busy for so long.

When I had realised that I could become a millionaire, I'd been compelled to go for it. Not for any other reason than I had wanted to achieve everything I was capable of achieving. I owed that to my parents in a way. I had started with nothing. My mum and dad had started with nothing. And I had always wanted to prove to them (and myself) that I could do it.

So we left Cheltenham straightaway and went back to see her. She could hear us talking to her but she couldn't say anything in response. She just moved her eyelids to demonstrate she could understand what I was saying to her. She died later that night. It was a blessing that she went like she did, I wouldn't have wanted her to suffer. She was eighty-two years old.

I owed a lot to my mum, not just to her much-vaunted luck, but to the way she treated people. She definitely passed that onto me too. I couldn't have done what I did, or achieved what I had without being a people-person too. I could have taken short cuts, or taken the cut-throat path to success, but that wouldn't have felt right. I owed it to my mum to do it right.

Dad ended up in hospital at the same time as my mum, but he held on a bit longer. He got better and they sent him to a home. I was angry with him after Mum died. He didn't go to her funeral, and I just thought he was being typically selfish. But then a psychologist friend of mine told me it probably wasn't that at all. He just couldn't face her funeral, the finality of it. He couldn't cope without my mum, and he spiralled down after that.

My dad – there was a man who could have done with some more luck! But his wife – my mum – had passed it all on to me! He used to do the football pools, week in, week out. He never really won anything, he was one of life's nearly-men punters. But then one year, they changed the rules. Before that, you needed twenty-four points to win the jackpot – eight draws of any score would do it. But after they changed, it, the eight draws all had to be score draws. There were three points for a score draw, and two points for a nil–nil.

The first week after it changed, he got eight draws. A week earlier, he would have scooped up the jackpot. He would have won about a hundred thousand pounds. He never stopped talking about how close he'd come.

He backed a dog once. He got a dead-cert tip and put five quid on it. It didn't win. He said, "I'll never back another dog ever again." And he never did. But it didn't matter how many times he lost on the horses, he kept on backing them. He loved it so much he was still putting bets on when he was on his death bed!

Like my mum, he'd had a heart attack, and he looked terrible that last day when we were with him in hospital. He leaned over to Colin – and I thought he might be about to say something profound to his grandson. Instead he said, "Where's the racing at tomorrow, Colin?" He knew I wouldn't have taken his bet. Dad had an account with our betting shop, and he'd ring up, and ask me, sheepishly, "Ron, what's my balance?" And I'd have a look and tell him it was fifteen pounds and twenty pence, and every single time he'd say, "Oh... I made it a bit more than that." But I'd give him short shrift, and he got fed up with me. So by the time Colin was working with me, he'd ring up and say, "It's only me, Ron, is Colin there?"

So Colin told him there was racing at Haydock Park, and my dad said, "Who's the top jockey riding there tomorrow?" And Colin told him it was Richard Hughes. So Dad said, "I'll have £1 cross, and £1 double on his first two rides." The first ride didn't win, but the second one came home in front. His last ever bet was a winner. He died before the result came in.

I think my dad would have taken a measure of pride in my success. More than that though, he'd have wanted his share of the credit. He would have said, I'd have never got into bookmaking if it hadn't been for him being a gambler! He knew how it worked. He knew he was always making a loss as a punter, and he knew where the money was really going – straight into the bookmaker's pockets. But he was more than pleased that I did what I did.

There was a moment with my dad towards the end that really summed him up. He looked up at me and said, "Ron, how can this happen to me?" He'd always thought he was invincible, he always thought he still had time. I knew I didn't want to go like that, feeling like I'd been hard done by, thinking that life had let me down.

CHAPTER ELEVEN

MY FRIENDS AND OTHER ANIMALS

As I think back over my working life, I'm always reminded of the people who helped make it so memorable. There was never any (serious) animosity between us, whichever side of the betting-shop counter we stood on, and Colin and I made some firm friends over the years.

A bookmaker making friends with punters?

It's true that bookmakers aren't generally liked by punters, but I'd discovered a long time ago that a happy punter made for a happy betting shop. Besides, I had my mother's gift for getting on with people, and I just couldn't help making friends!

I've had plenty of thoughts about who I'd cast as the revolving cast of people that came into our shops and into our lives over the years. There were some right characters among them. Freddie Wray was a farrier in Newmarket. He was a conscientious worker; he'd be there at the stables at four in the morning, every morning, and he loved what he did. He shod Teenoso, the Derby winner, in 1983, trained by Geoff Wragg. He told me he was working in the yard when 'Wraggy' came out of the house looking chuffed to bits. He said, "I've got Lester to ride the horse!"

"Lester..." he said. "You do mean Lester Pigott?"

Geoff nodded happily, and Freddie told him, "I'll be back in half an hour." He was off down the bookies to put £200 on Teenoso at 16/1!

Freddie was a good friend, and a great bloke to have a drink and a meal with; whenever we ate out, he always came and sat next to me. He wasn't just a farrier though, Fred was a gambler too, and that's how I got to know him. A pal of mine was selling his betting shop and offered me four of his accounts. He'd not exactly been firm with his punters and had let them build up some substantial debts. That wasn't my way of working – it was either pay-as-you-play, or pay within seven days – so I asked him two key questions. "Do they lose? And do they pay?"

He ummed and ahhed a bit, but I took on the four of them anyway, and one of those was Fred's account. The other three lasted less than two months, but Freddie... The first bet he had with me was a £5 Lucky 15 and a £10 each way Accumulator. The first horse in the list won at 33/1, and he had £340 going on the second horse. If that had won, we might have had a very short friendship! But he didn't take the shirt off my back that day, and he built up a good account with me over the years. He was a very trusting chap too. He used to ring me up and say, "What do I owe you, Ron? About £700 is it?"

And I'd say, "It's actually a bit more than that, Freddie. It's a thousand."

"Oh, okay, I thought it might be a bit more, no problem. I'll put the cash in the post to you." Then he would wrap up the bank notes in newspaper, and put them in an unregistered envelope and pop them in the post box. I'd get the letter, open up the newspaper and find a big bundle of cash inside!

We went to pick him up from his flat in Newmarket one time, and we were running late. We'd booked a table for 7.00 p.m., and we were still five miles away. So I jumped out of the taxi and went to get him. But he sounded agitated. "Ron, you need to come in, you need to see this..."

Reluctantly, I agreed to go in and went up to his flat. He let me in and hurried me over to his computer. There was one window open on the screen... a Russian Brides website! "Look at this, Ron, she's a nurse in Russia."

"She's gorgeous, Freddie... But what about this meal we're late for?"

Freddie didn't have food on his mind! "Ron, she's coming to see me. I've sent her £500 for the air fare." You can guess the rest! Fred never did have a wife – Russian or otherwise. That was one gamble that Fred didn't win, and there were others.

Freddie didn't just like to bet on the horses, he bet at the casinos too, and he would even chance his arm at the infamous Odd or Even game. That's one you might not have heard of, so let me explain...

I'd take a £20 note out of my pocket and casually say, "Alright, Fred, last digit on the serial number... odd or even?" If he guessed it right, I had to give him the twenty. Now, I stress to you, in black and white, that there was no cheating whatsoever, but I used to empty his pocket every time we played, and being a gambler, he couldn't stop himself from playing. It got to the point where he'd come in saying, "I'm not playing, Ron! Let's just have a drink." Ten minutes later, he'd say, "Go on, get the money out." He couldn't help himself.

Freddie got his revenge though, just not in the way he expected. We were in Newmarket to see Choisir, the first horse that had won two races in the same week at Royal Ascot. It was a big, hulking sprinter and it had won both the sprints that week with ease. The trainer took it to Newmarket for the July Cup, and it was stabled at Geoff Wragg's place. Freddie told us, "You should come and see this horse. It's not a race horse, it's an elephant!"

Sure enough, I had never seen a horse as big in my life. And still to this day, I have never seen a bigger horse. It was a beast of an animal. I had been around horses often enough to know how to approach them, and I reached out to stroke its nose when, quick as you like it took a piece of my finger!

"You bastard!" I was hopping from foot to foot in pain, incensed by the thing. But I knew how to get my revenge. It was favourite to win at Newmarket so I decided that I would lay Choisir, it meant that, favourite or not, I would stand to lose the absolute maximum if the finger-biter won his next race. It came in second. (I don't think it lost by as much as a length; more like, it lost by a finger!)

We were always surprised that Freddie never had any tips for us. Considering all the people he was working with down at Newmarket, and all the insight he had, you'd think he would have been full of tips. But no. He'd never tip a horse. Well, almost never...

One night, Freddie mentioned a horse being trained by Geoff Wragg, and we had never heard him talk about a horse like that before. He couldn't say enough good things about it. He was telling us, "This could be the best filly he'd ever had."

The horse was Heron Bay, and Freddie told us she was running at Chester the next week in a maiden race; so we should have a few quid each way. It finished second at 9/1. Next, it ran at Haydock, where it was the 7/4 joint favourite and ran an absolute stinker. But Freddie was adamant: Heron Bay was on the verge of winning. Then it ran in the Britannia Handicap at Royal Ascot. It was 25/1 that day. A pal of ours, Peter McGrane, had a thousand quid each way on her. He won thirty thousand quid that day. Heron Bay paid for his wedding!

Peter always used to surprise us. He came to Royal Ascot one week and just disappeared. We were there for the week and on the first day of racing he just didn't turn up. It transpired that he'd been in the hotel bar at midnight, talking to a guy who had a horse running in Chantilly in France the next day, but didn't have anyone to go with. Full of alcohol, Peter said, "You have got someone to go with; I'm coning with you." That was Pete all over. Impulsive.

We were in Listowel, late one morning, heading out for lunch, when who should we see but Peter, coming up the street towards us with a pint of Guinness in his hands! Even though he was walking straight towards us, he was oblivious to us being there. "Peter!" I yelled.

He seemed excited to see us. "Hello, Ron! Hello, Colin," he sang as he swayed towards us.

"You're starting early aren't you, Peter?"

"No, Ron – I'm finishing late!"

Horse Racing Ireland wouldn't let him bet that day for obvious reasons.

I was never a particularly big drinker, but we inevitably spent quite a bit of time in pubs, and there were certainly some serious drinkers in our crowd. But the people we mixed with were big personalities, and just as gregarious with or without a drink in their hands. To some of them, drinking came as naturally as breathing. It was part of the environment they'd grown up in, and no one thought too seriously about getting old or getting ill. There were some loud nights and some bad hangovers, but we were surrounded by friendly, generous people, and every night out brought its own unique possibilities.

For example, we were in a pub in Newmarket one night when Peter came in, breathless with excitement. "We've just bought a racehorse," he announced. "And you each owe me twelve hundred guineas for your share."

Despite all my years in the game, I had never been offered a share in a racehorse before, and I'd certainly never expected to be offered a quarter of a horse on a night out in the pub. It wasn't the kind of proposition any of us had expected to hear that night, but it was all part and parcel of being friends with Peter. You never quite knew what he was going to get up to next.

I'd had greyhounds, of course, but never seriously considered getting a share in a racehorse because I knew it was an altogether more complicated (and costly) business. It was two thousand pounds a month back then to train a horse. But when you've had a few drinks, and you're presented with an opportunity like that, it suddenly sounds as if it might be worth a punt.

Peter had acquired the five thousand guinea filly at the yearling sales at Newmarket, from a racecourse trainer (who shall remain anonymous) who'd had a horse called Send In The Tank, that had been a prolific winner. So we decided to call our filly Sendinpost. Although the breeding was good, it didn't have the best legs apparently, but I stumped up the cash for my share regardless, and Colin and Fred got in on it too.

We left Sendinpost with the same trainer; we knew he was a pretty shrewd guy. He ran the horse in three races as a two-year-old, but didn't try to win any of them. It meant we had a better horse than its handicap mark suggested.

Then it ran in a nursery handicap in Windsor, while we were over at the Galway Festival. It opened at odds of 4/1 and drifted like a barge to 10/1. We got Peter on the phone to the trainer before the race to see if it was time to make an investment. The trainer said he wouldn't bother; he expected her to run well, but she wouldn't win the race.

We didn't back it and, of course, our horse won the race. We'd have had a nice little return on that, even if we'd only put fifty quid a piece on it.

Sendinpost ran again a month or so later at Kempton. It opened up at 13/2 and then went down to 4/1. "She's still not ready," he told us. "Don't waste your money." It won again.

That was the final straw, as far as we were concerned. The horse was costing us about five hundred quid a month each, and we had nothing to show for it. Somebody might have been doing very nicely off the back of our investment, but it wasn't us.

We took the horse out of his yard and put it back in the sales. With a couple of wins to her name, we got forty grand for it, and considered ourselves well shot of the thing. It went on to run as a hurdler, but failed at the fences, and ended up being sold for eight thousand quid.

After Sendinpost, even Peter mellowed. He had always been a bit of Jack-the-lad, and as flighty as a balloon, but he seemed to settle happily into married life – and then fatherhood. I hadn't seen him for a while, and then one day, there was a knock at my door. Lo-and-behold it was Peter with a baby in his arms. This was something I hadn't ever thought I'd see, Peter with a baby. I was happy to see him, albeit surprised. So of course I let him in, he plonked the baby down onto the floor and changed her nappy like someone who'd done it a hundred times before. I couldn't quite believe what I was seeing. It turns out that he'd brought his wife and his mother-in-law over to Chester for a long weekend, and they'd gone out shopping and he'd come to see me instead.

In some ways, seeing Peter handling dirty nappies with ease was stranger than seeing him careering down the street in a morning with a pint in hand, or propositioning us with the chance to buy a share in a horse. When he'd finished, he threw me the dirty nappy and said cheerfully, "Here, you know what to do with that!"

I got my own back on him later, and it was the old Odd and Even game that did it! There were four of his lot and four of mine, out on the town in Tralee. I could see the meal was going to stack up to be five hundred quid or more. We could have split the bill, but where's the fun in that? I told him we'd decide who paid on a single round of the game, and said, "Do you feel lucky, punk?"

He was in. Now the thing with Peter is that he always chose odd, and I knew that. It would have been so easy to rig it, but I wouldn't ever have done that. I put my hand in my pocket, pulled out a twenty and said, "What have we got?"

"That's like you, Ron," he said. "It's odd and you're odd!"

"Are you sure about that, Peter?" I said, holding up the note. "Is four an odd number?"

He got his Barclaycard out and paid for the meal!

***

Then there was Tony – he's part of our team to this day. A quick-witted Scouser – don't tell him, I said that – who's a bit of a history specialist. (You have to be to support Everton!)

When we started buying up pitches in earnest, we spirited Tony onto our team. In the politest way possible, we knew he'd been about a bit professionally, and he knew what he was doing. He'd had a betting shop of his own, but had spent most of his working life on the course. We'd got to know him at Chester. Tony would come and hedge a bet with us, and we liked him straightaway. He had a good way with the punters too. So when his old boss was starting to fall out of love with the game we came in with an offer for him.

Like us, I felt that Tony had a winning way about him. I don't just mean he was a good bookmaker; he was (and is). I mean that he had a winning way with people, and I wanted everyone associated with Ron Wadey Racing to exemplify that in their dealings with the punters. I think my mother would have expected that of me.

***

We had a pal called Joe Haran, also known as Smoking Joe, also known as Irish Joe. He was a bit of a character, mad as a hatter. He was another old punter from the shop days. We used to go to the pub with him sometimes, and after a drink, he'd go round shaking everyone's hand.

We'd rented some houses for a race meeting one time, and we ended up on the same estate with him. Joe used to pop in and bring the Racing Post. Now, Tony was a dab hand at mimicking the old trim phone bbrring-bbrring, and when Joe came into the house, Tony would duck out of sight and start whistling like a phone. Of course, I'd be too busy to answer and I'd say, "Get that would you, Joe." Then Joe would look about him helplessly, as the ringing continued.

"Ron! I can't find the phone!"

He unexpectedly got his own back at Cheltenham. He rang me up to ask where we were staying for the Festival. He'd found himself a nice place in a hotel in Cirencester, just a few miles outside Cheltenham, and rang me to recommend it. He sold me on the idea and I booked a twin rom for me and Colin.

After the racing on the Tuesday, we got back, and we saw there was water drip, drip, dripping from the chandelier on the ceiling. I told the receptionist on our way to dinner, and when we got back later that evening, it had got much worse.

Nobody had come to check it out, but we turned in and hoped it would peter out. It didn't.

DRIP! DRIP! DRIP!

It was like water torture, so I got back on the phone and told the receptionist that they'd need to find us another room.

There was a pause. "I'm sorry, sir, all the other rooms are occupied... all except one." The hotel was being redecorated and there was a room at the far end that was waiting to be seen to. "It hasn't been used for months, I'm afraid it might be a bit musty."

I didn't care. It was after midnight, and I just wanted to get out of that noise. So I grabbed my blazer and stuffed all my money in the inside pockets. "We'll come back for our stuff in the morning," I told Colin. So in boxer shorts and blazer, I followed the receptionist half way across Cirencester – or at least that's what it felt like! Five minutes later, we arrived at the room. It was musty. It was cold. But at least it was quiet!

There was just one problem. It's all very well traipsing through a hotel in your boxer shorts at past-midnight, but we hadn't given a thought to going back for all of our belongings the next morning. At eight in the morning we set off back to our original room, and the hotel was alive and buzzing with people. In a blazer stuffed with money, no shirt, and no trousers I must have looked quite the sight as people were emerging from their rooms for breakfast!

I still see Joe around and about. He lives in Warrington and whenever I see him, I can still hear Tony making that ringing sound.

***

There's just one problem with friends though, isn't there? Sooner or later, one way or another, you have to say goodbye to them.

Freddie is another in the long list of people I've known who have died from cancer. He was just forty-nine years of age. He was diagnosed in October 2009, and died in January 2010. I went to see him in hospital after Christmas, and I hardly recognised him. He'd gone from about thirteen stone down to six. He was wasting away.

I was heading out to Australia for three weeks for the tennis, and looking at him, I knew I wouldn't see him again. I got up to leave and said, "I'll see you when I'm back, Fred," knowing full well that I wouldn't.

"Ron," he said, "hug me."

I put my arms around him and cried.

He was a cracking bloke, Freddie. Everyone loved him; the church was rammed for his funeral. There'll never be another one like him.

CHAPTER TWELVE

ADVENTURES IN IRELAND

I was going out with a woman called Marjorie, who lived in County Kildare. As well as finding me irresistible, she was a great tennis player too. So it was an ideal match! By the time we went our separate ways, she might even have been a better player than me!

I was making more frequent trips to Ireland for the racing, so I decided to get a place of my own out there. I just couldn't find anywhere that was quite right. I was out in Wexford buying a greyhound puppy, and as well as the puppy, I bought myself an acre of land in Enniscorthy, County Wexford. (I must have been spending too much time with Peter McGrane to do something so impulsive!) But when I saw the plot up for sale, it made sense. I'd always wanted to build a house of my own. Marjorie had a cousin who was influential in the planning department and helped me get the permission to build the house.

It was a four-bedroom house, set in landscaped gardens. I kitted it out with a Jacuzzi bath, and an Aga, and of course I put in a tennis court. I even put in underfloor heating throughout... Now that was expensive, but not as expensive as guests! One night after Punchestown Races, when Colin and Tony were staying with me, we came back in and Colin had left his lights on all day. I gave him a good talking to about that.

Breakfast was not provided for my electricity-wasting guests, but I knew a good pub in Moone, on the way to the races. The first day we turned up, and the village idiot was holding court. We were so impressed by him that we had to go back and see him again the next day! Peter, his name was, and he was a big, fat chap and had an opinion on anything and everything. Inevitably, we got talking about football.

"Who's your team, Peter?" I asked. "Chelsea," he told us. They were on their way to winning the Premier League at the time.

Tony asked him, "Have you been to Stamford Bridge?"

"No," said Peter, "But I've been past it!"

After we let that sink in, he went on, "I'll tell you a team that'll go well next season," he said. We waited to hear what he had to say...

"Birmingham."

Next season Birmingham were relegated back to the Championship!

John, the landlord was a bit of a character too. In among all the usual country pub paraphernalia on the walls were several pictures of Clint Eastwood. And in one of the pictures, he was standing next to John. It turned out that Clint had gone to the pub, with his entourage in tow, for drinks in an authentic Irish pub, in between rounds of golf. The story went that he'd been preceded into the pub by one of his entourage who'd informed John, "We've got a VIP outside, is it alright if he comes in?" The pub was empty.

At that, John said straight-faced, "Anybody who walks through that door is a VIP."

"Yeah, but this is Clint Eastwood."

"Anybody who walks through that door is a VIP!"

The news had spread fast through the village, and within ten minutes, everyone was there. "Clint Eastwood is buying drinks for everybody!"

At that, Peter piped up, "Yeah he came in as Clint Eastwood, he went out as *Skint* Eastwood!"

That was Peter all over. He cracked us up. When he went up to the bar to pay for his breakfast, he pulled a fistful of change (not dollars) out of his pocket, threw it on the counter, and told the poor girl working behind the bar, "No need to check that, I'm a well-respected man in these parts!" The poor girl was Polish, she didn't have a clue what he was on about. And then he added, "Oh, and by the way, I've only had a mini-size breakfast, not like these lads with their big plates of breakfast." Given half a chance he looked like he would have had a sausage off our plates as soon as look at us. Peter seemed to be in an awful hurry and as he was leaving he said, "I've got to go and put the chops on for my lunch!" I think it's fair to say that he was a bit of a grubber!

We wanted to find out more about Peter, and sure enough, he was there ahead of us again the next morning, glad to have another audience. They served two types of breakfast – a full Irish breakfast or a mini. Peter had been in a while before us and already polished off his own breakfast. He had eyes like saucers when our three breakfasts arrived. He shouted across to the bar, "Excuse me, how come they've got mushrooms?"

The landlord's wife was behind the bar and said, wearily, "We're saving your mushrooms to go with the steaks tonight!"

Eleven o'clock came and went, and I said to Peter, "I thought you said you started work at the petrol station at eleven?"

"I do," he said.

"Well, it's ten past."

"So what?" he retorted.

I said, "I'm glad you don't work for me."

Quick as a flash he came right back at me, "*I'm* glad I don't work for you!"

Peter disappeared out of the pub and out of our lives that morning. We completed our work at Punchestown that week and all went back to England. A little while later, I was back in Wexford, and as I arrived at the house, Colin's light was shining out to greet me. It had been on for two months! I had more words with him after that!

I may not have been the most generous-hearted host, but I'll tell you one thing about the Irish: they're generous to a fault. On one occasion, after I'd flown back to England so I could get to Sandown the next day, Colin and Tony got stranded in Dublin. I'll own up to this one: I sent them the wrong way to the port. So Colin called on Peter McGrane up in Drogheda – the lad who'd won his wedding money on Heron Bay – and he got them a bed for the night, he got them a meal; they didn't want for anything.

Peter came down to play tennis with me in Wexford sometimes too. (Really he came down for a drink, but we played a bit of tennis too.) We'd just got to one of my favourite pubs one day – it was a good half-hour away, but the excellent fish made it worthwhile. We'd just arrived one day when my alarm went off. Something was wrong back at the house. I was all for going back, but Peter, with the scent of beer in his nostrils now – told me to ring John, the man I'd bought the land from.

So I got on the phone and John's wife, Ruth, answered. She used to swear like an absolute trooper!

"Ruth," I started, "The alarm's gone off."

"Ah, it'll be fucking nothing!" she said! "Don't you be worried about that."

I persevered. "Can you go and check it for me please?"

"Will I bollocks go and check it" she came back. And that was that. I ate my fish and tried not to worry about whatever had tripped the alarm back at home.

But that was the problem with being out in the middle of nowhere – the loneliest part of nowhere! Sometimes I'd be rolling around on my own in the big house. Not much point having a tennis court if you haven't even got anybody to return your serves! So it was bad enough by day, but lonelier still at night. I remember one night sitting bolt upright in bed. Outside it was pitch black, but I had heard the tell-tale crunch of car tyres on the gravel driveway. It was so quiet out there and if anyone ever came to the house, day or night, you could hear them as soon as they turned onto the long drive. Sure enough, the glow of the headlights played across my bedroom wall.

I was straight on the phone to John; I knew he had a double-barrelled shotgun. Fortunately, it was him – not Ruth – who answered the phone in the dead of night. Then the car's headlights went out and the sound of the engine died down. Silence. Then there was a loud knock at the door. I could see the shape of the man through my bedroom window and the shape of the double-barrelled shotgun. It was John. So together we went out to face them – whoever they were. The guy in the front of the car said something about looking for a party; well they certainly weren't having a party at my house! And by the time they caught sight of the double-barrelled shotgun, they went looking for their party elsewhere!

But having built the house, I felt obliged to use it, so I would go over whenever I had any free time, even if I was on my own. Whenever I got there, the first thing I'd do was inspect the tennis court. Every single time, the rabbits had crapped all over it. It was an AstroTurf surface so you couldn't brush it off, it would just embed itself deeper into the surface. So no sooner had I arrived than I'd be on my knees, rubber gloves on, picking up those little black pellets. It took hours!

So, I was ready to sell after all of that. I'd put a lot of time and money into making the house as good as it could, and fortunately the estate agents agreed with me. They praised its exceptional architectural design! And luckily enough, someone came up to me at Galway Races and said he knew someone that wanted to buy it and she had the money. Or her sugar daddy had the money! And they paid the full asking price. I got speaking to him – he was a nice guy – and he'd noticed the tennis court. So he said he'd throw in a couple of tickets for the Wednesday of the second week – men's quarter final day at Wimbledon.

The house sold in October 2007, and then the following January, the property market just collapsed. They must have lost about two hundred grand on that house in the space of a couple of months. I had got out at just the right time once again. More importantly though, what about those promised tickets? He rang me a little later and I said, "I didn't think I'd hear from you again!" But true to his word, he sent me the promised tickets.

In the end, Marjorie and I went our separate ways. But we'd enjoyed our time together, travelling the world and watching the tennis. And, although I may have lost the girl, at least I got the men's quarter final tickets!

CHAPTER THIRTEEN

PITCH PERFECT

I'd decided to give up on the greyhounds precisely because I'd been so lucky. Too lucky! I hadn't spent very much money on them, but they'd brought in some big wins, and I thought, *It can't go on like this. Lightning won't strike twice.* Maybe I didn't want to push my mother's luck too far? So I jumped ship.

The bookmaking business is where my heart lay anyway, and I built up the on-course business in just the same way as I'd built up the shop portfolio. With Colin and Tony, we started out with some fair pitches, did as much as we could with them, and then moved up to better pitches in better locations.

We started building up the portfolio quickly with good pitches at Aintree, Ascot, Brighton, Bangor, Cartmel, Cheltenham, Chester, Epsom, Fontwell, Newmarket, Sandown, Sedgefield and Uttoxeter. By the time we were in full flow, it was widely known that Ron Wadey was in the market for racecourse pitches. I was on holiday in Torquay, where a guy lived who was to sell me my next Royal Ascot pitch, and we played some tennis. Afterwards, I just happened to drop into Newton Abbot races; it would have felt wrong not to. The TV anchor was interviewing people going into the track, and when I casually walked across the shot, she beckoned me over and said, "What brought you to the races today, sir?"

I said, "My car," and walked off.

There would have been a few people seeing me there and wondering what I was doing at Newton Abbot racecourse. Some of them would have thought I had a betting coup on the go. Some of them would have thought: *There goes Ron, buying up some more pitches.*

It wasn't just about the pitches though, we picked the right people to work with us, especially when we expanded our portfolio to Ireland.

When I first started working on the courses in Ireland, I was the first English bookmaker to do it successfully. A few others followed, but a lot more have fallen by the wayside. And I had to rely on the kindness of new friends to help me do it. Justin Flood has been a cracking friend and ally. He and his dad were always extremely helpful. Some of the Irish bookmakers resented me, but not those guys. Brian Keenan and his son – also Brian – gave us so much support and kindness, and we couldn't have made our way into the Irish scene without having Ray and Seamus Mulvaney to help us. We went into partnership with them at Chester and Newmarket, where we bet under the name Seamus Mulvaney.

I don't think Seamus would mind me calling him a good old curmudgeon, but he's a much-loved personality in the industry. For his seventieth birthday, all the bookmakers arranged a party for Seamus in a nice hotel in Galway. It was all paid for. There must have been a hundred people there. He never turned up! He hates birthdays.

I still wanted to celebrate with Seamus though. So, far from the madding crowd, I went to see him, and I had two envelopes for him. In one envelope, there was some money that I owed him. Quite a lot of money, actually, but he didn't even bother to count it, he just put it straight in his inside pocket. (Bookmakers are supposed to be tight-fisted, un-trusting types, but when you find a good 'un, you know you can trust them to the ends of the earth.)

There was one envelope left, and he eyed it suspiciously.

"It's something for your big day," I said. Now I'd been careful and bought him a sixtieth birthday card instead of a seventieth, just to be polite. But he took it out of my hand, ripped it in half and threw it straight on the floor! I've never tried to celebrate another birthday with him ever since!

All of these people went above and beyond in making us all feel welcome. And it's in no small part thanks to them that we feel like we're part of the furniture over there now. We've proved ourselves to the local bookmaking fraternity, and they treat us like one of their own.

That doesn't mean I always win in Ireland though! I had my worst ever day at Punchestown Races in Ireland. I lost twenty-five grand in one day and did nothing wrong. Every favourite won that day. To make matters worse, I couldn't get any more money sent across to me for forty-eight hours, and that's when I had to rely on my friends again. Dennis Deane and Peter McGrane both gave me five thousand, just so I could trade. At the end of the five-day festival, I'd won eighteen grand back, and under the circumstances, I was quite pleased with that.

You've got to have nerves of steel to make a go of it in this game. Colin used to be close to tears when we lost, and I had to tell him: If it's going to make you feel like that, you need to go and get another job. Fortunately, that was one time he did listen to me!

It was just as well too, because there were days you could get wiped out, and finish up with nothing to show for it. Royal Ascot in 2010 springs to mind. We'd had a terrible time of it. We'd made no money, and we only just about scraped our expenses. We went home with our tails between our legs that time, and went back to Brighton on the Monday afternoon, hoping that we'd fare a little better. There wasn't a soul in site, and I knew I was going to have a hard time making any money that day.

I was about to give it up as a bad idea when I looked at my screen and saw a horse called Stargazer – a 20/1 chance. It was what we called a 'taker'. It wouldn't win me any money, but it wouldn't lose me anything either. But if a 20/1 horse was going to win, then I knew I needed to be backing it. So I decided to put £50 on Stargazer for a potential £1,000 return. But there was a problem. I didn't press the

£50 button... I pressed the £500 button. Suddenly a bad day and a bad week were looking a whole lot worse.

But by the time I realised, they were already off – it was only a sprint – and it was late to do anything except grit my teeth and wait for the inevitable.... Except that the horse won. And I won £10,000 by default. I was practically doing somersaults. My mother's luck again!

It's always an interesting meeting; they have a ladies' day at Brighton, and a lot of ladies do go... but a lot of transvestites go too! We had an Irishman called Jimmy Dunne working with us one year and he took a good look around and said, "I'm seventy years old, and I've never seen anything like it in my life!" You could see the look of horror on his face when he came out of the men's toilets followed by a man dressed like a woman!

So I took to the on-track way of life like a duck to water! Especially in Galway – where it almost always rained! I remember the Galway Festival in 2012. On the first day, we sat in the car and the rain was lashing down, rain like you wouldn't believe! It was bouncing off the Tarmac.

I didn't want to take a chance on the computer equipment getting wet, because if it did get wet, and then it stopped working, we'd have been stuck. I didn't want to take a chance on missing the big day on Thursday, so I said, "That's it. Let's got to the pub!" I'd never, ever done that before. I'd never abandoned a meeting, but we went to the pub, desperately hoping that all the favourites were going to win!

We had a few pints and watched the racing. I was in bed by eight o'clock. The rain was bad enough, but being stuck in the pub with Tony, talking about Everton for hours on end... that was really tough! But we had a good time. We made the best of it, and we enjoyed some good trips to Ireland. It wasn't just about the racing anymore. We were enjoying the occasions, and the banter in the betting ring. It was all good craic! I don't think I'd have carried on so long if I hadn't been able to enjoy the experience of being a bookmaker. You show me a bookmaker who tells you he's only in it for the money, and I'll show you a man without too many friends in the racing fraternity. And that would have never been the life for me.

There was something else I liked about Galway. It was the allure of the promised land behind the exclusive entrance to the Mayor's Garden...

Like most racecourses, Galway had a main betting ring, a grandstand, and at the other end of the grandstand, there's the Mayor's Garden. That's where the margins were greater than those in the main betting ring, and I wanted in. There were, of course, places available at a price – there always are – and I deemed it a price worth paying. Getting in gave you access to a different clientele, with elevated spending power, but you had to be a bit canny. On a ten-horse race, we might have been betting to 125% in the Mayor's Garden, but in the ring, they'd be betting to around 115%. So I used to put a man in the main ring with a walkie talkie, and I'd be on the other end saying, "What price number 3? I've just laid 5/1 for £500." (That was worth two and a half grand, but in the ring it would be on at 7/1, for winnings of two thousand.) So I had to weigh up the reduced winnings value versus the value of bets I'd be taking and make sure I ended up on the right side of the thin black line between profit and loss.

I think I judged it pretty well. We still used money satchels back then to store our float and our takings, and one day in the Mayor's Garden, I could not squeeze one more £10 note into mine. It was literally overflowing. In the end, we were just stuffing the surplus notes into a carrier bag!

I had a pitch at Punchestown in the hospitality suite too. We paid four or five grand for the privilege but it was worth it. We had to use the same odds in Corporate Hospitality as they did in the ring, so the margins weren't that great. I had a mediocre pitch in the ring, so I set Colin and Tony up in corporate, with our friend, Johnny Egg, as we called him. They were getting wined and dined, and enjoying all the benefits of corporate hospitality. Tony came out after the first race and looked well fed.

"What's it like in there?" I asked him slightly enviously.

"Have you ever been to Butlins, Ron?" he said with a wink.

Johnny could eat for Ireland, and was stopping the girls going by with their trollies.

"Another cup of tea over here, love. Any cake with that? We'll take three dinners now, please..."

Another Irish grubber! We were in Stratford with John for the Cheltenham Festival. We'd booked a nice restaurant, and we got there early, but I was absolutely parched, so we nipped into a Wetherspoons across the road. We settled in at the bar and I ordered myself a pint of Guinness. John had long since stopped drinking and just had a pint of orange juice. He was more interested in the waitresses passing by with big plates of dinner.

"Ron," he said, "why don't we eat in here?"

I downed my pint and dragged him out before he started ordering up bar snacks.

We were in a pub in Galway with him another time. We'd both ordered fillet steaks and his came first. It looked like a six-ouncer, I could see him sizing it up. And then out came my fillet steak, and mine looked like an eight-ouncer.

His hand shot up. "Excuse me, ma'am, can you tell me why his steak is bigger than mine?"

But I said, "John, I'm paying the bill, that's why my steak's bigger than yours!"

***

So we'd been accepted by the Irish, we'd got some good pitches on both sides of the Irish Sea, and we'd started making some good money. There was just one problem – getting the money back into England from Ireland back in the days when bookmaking was a cash-only business!

We were coming back from a successful meeting at Listowel, flying out of Shannon Airport into Stanstead, and then on to Newmarket. Now one of the most famous Irish jockeys of the time happened to be on the plane with us that day, and there was a bit of controversy around him over allegations of race fixing, and the British tabloids were all over him.

The flight was a bit of a free-for-all. You got on and sat wherever you liked, or wherever you could find a seat if you got on late. We were all done up in our formal best and looking smart. We were at either end of a row of three, thinking that everyone had boarded and no one was going to sit between us when this diminutive figure got on with a big bruiser behind him. It was him.

He looked around for somewhere to sit, clocked that there was a space between us and came and sat down next to us. He settled himself down then turned and fixed me with a stare.

"I'll make your life easy for you," he said.

"What do you mean?" I asked. I knew who it was, of course. Some bookmaker I'd have been if I hadn't known him. But I had no idea what he was on about.

"You're watching me, aren't you. Doing a surveillance on me."

His mate walked by and said in an audible whisper, "Kieren, there's a seat over here."

"No, you go on," he said. "I'm fine here next to the two police officers!"

"Behave yourself!" I retorted. "I'm not police."

He wasn't discouraged. "Well, if you're not, he is," he said pointing to Colin.

Things got a little bit more complicated for him in the next few months I'm afraid to say, when the real police got involved. But for us, leaving Ireland was almost always with a sense of a job well done and, sometimes, more money than we could carry...

We used to wear money belts, so I went through customs with twenty thousand in my money belt! Colin had about the same. I walked straight through, looked over my shoulder to say something to Colin and there was no sign of him.

He'd been pulled into the office, and all I could think about was our hard-earned money getting confiscated. They might have pegged him as a drug dealer. I had to rely on Colin to charm them with an explanation, and they duly let him go.

Perhaps he's inherited a bit of his grandmother's luck.

We've certainly had some adventures over the years, and we've taken a few diversions into unfamiliar territory. But it doesn't always pay to be an innovator!

I enjoyed a fair few tennis holidays after my so-called retirement, and I'd met a very pleasant lady called Jo Graham. We bonded over our love of tennis, and it turned out that we had a mutual interest in the horses too, although you might say we moved in different circles; while I was a bookmaker, Jo was an international judge on the dressage circuit. But credit to Jo – and I really must give her the credit here because I don't want it – she came up with the interesting suggestion that we should manage a betting facility at a dressage meeting near Congleton in Cheshire.

I didn't have a clue about dressage, and neither did Colin. We didn't even have the foggiest idea about how to price an event up, but we were game for a laugh, and decided to give it a go. Nothing ventured...

We met Jo the day before the event, and she told us the dressage crowd would back the rider more than the horse, particularly Olympic medallists Carl Hester and Charlotte Dujardin. So she 'marked our card' as to who would be regarded as the favourites, and who would be considered the outsiders.

There were two main events, the Open and the Grand Prix. We played it cagey on the first event. Not wanting to get our fingers burned, we opened up joint favourites 5/4 'each of two,' 11/8 bar! There was a plentiful crowd that day, but it's fair to say that we stuck out like an old nag in the rarefied atmosphere of the dressage crowd, and business was, to put it mildly, dire.

We were struggling to stay awake, when three ladies made a beeline for the pitch, and one of them said, "Ooh, Debbie is 33/1, I'll have a fiver each way!"

She was quickly joined by the second lady, and then the third. It was a fiver each way all round. With tickets in hand, Debbie's fan club made their way to the public stand to wait for their hero to take to the arena and win them a little extra spending money. Or potentially, a lot of spending money, actually. We'd taken £30, but if their faith in Debbie was rewarded and she put in the performance of a lifetime, we were going to lose around £600.

Suddenly we were wide awake, and getting more interested in dressage by the moment. Debbie was fifteenth in line to compete, and by the time she took to the arena, even I was convinced she was going to win! But you don't beat this old bookmaker quite so easily. There was a large metal gate to the side of the arena, and I'd thought how distracting it would be for horse and rider if somebody were to walk over there and carelessly open and shut it a few times. Colin was the man for the job, obviously. I had a reputation to maintain!

The cheers that greeted the arrival of Debbie into the ring were soon drowned out by Colin's disgraceful noise over at the gate.

Now, I wouldn't have known a good score from a bad one earlier that day, but by that stage I felt like an expert. The current leader was Carl Hester with an excellent score of 78.5%, but would Debbie beat it? As she completed her round, all eyes turned to the scoreboard. Colin had finally finished his gate solo, and an expectant hush descended over the crowd...

64.5%...

I looked over to Colin and gave him a big thumbs up. Job done! To celebrate, we had a couple of burgers, and an ice cream each. Cost: £30.

"Put it down to expenses," I said.

There were two days of dressage at Congleton. There were no bookmakers present for the second day!

Back on more familiar territory, we were in Aintree for the 2017 Grand National. There were a hundred and fifty thousand people there, including, so it seemed, the entire population of Scotland. I'd got a good friend of mine, Pat Brandon, to come up from London to help us out over the three days.

Patsy, as I like to call him, had worked regularly for us at various southern racecourses for a few years. Everyone seems to know Pat, he's a really likeable chap, but as one fellow bookmaker once put it, "He's a good fella to have on your side if there's any bother!" Pat could most definitely take care of it.

After the first race of the day, one of the thousands of Scots in attendance approached the pitch where I was working with Pat, and handed over what he thought was a winning ticket. I looked at the ticket, scanned it, and the payout display on the laptop read: Not a winner.

"Nothing on that, sir," I informed the punter.

"You sure about that?"

"Yes," I told him, "It didn't win."

The rather bemused and unhappy gentleman turned and walked back in the direction he'd come from, and something told me that wasn't the last I was going to see of him that day. Sure enough, seven races and – so it seemed to me – copious amounts of alcohol later, he was back, ticket in hand, and wife at his side.

"'Hey! Ye said there wisnae anything back on ma ticket, it's a fucking winner."

On scanning the ticket a second time, the display did indeed show that there was a return of £45. A bit bemused, I could only apologise. I told him I was very sorry, and that the scanner did sometimes malfunction.

"It's £45, here's £50 for your trouble," I said placatingly.

Through slightly gritted teeth, I handed over five ten-pound notes, but he didn't want to give up and go so quietly. Bookmakers, we're a much maligned and sometimes hated breed! I took the tirade of abuse that followed – I'd heard worse. But it was clear he wanted to take things to the next level – he was up for a scrap. And that's when Pat stepped in.

"Look, mate," he said, calm as you like. "He's given you £50 and he's apologised, mistakes happen." He paused a moment or two to size up the irate punter, who was looking a lot less sure of himself. "Now Ron pays out the money, that's his department... But if anyone gets aggressive and wants a fight, that's my department."

The punter considered his options. Of all the bets he'd made that day, he'd have been onto a loser taking on our Patsy. By this time, his wife had obviously observed that Pat was probably quite handy in his 'department' and realised that her husband would almost certainly have come off second best had things escalated any further. She whisked him away for another drink.

So I put that one down to a ghost in the machine, and I have Pat to thank for his very timely intervention. You certainly have to be able to think fast in this game, and it's good to know I can rely on my friends. But sometimes, it's just me and my mother's luck...

I was having an uneventful Listowel. The bets had been moderate at best, and our takings had been nothing to write home about. A race was about to go off, and I had my head stuck in the computer, when a punter came in with a bet for five hundred Euros on a 14/1 chance; horse number twelve. I took the bet, but no sooner had I done it than the alarm bells started ringing, I was set to lose two thousand Euros if it won.

I shot off to a pal of mine, Martin McGarrity, to try and hedge the bet. By the time I reached him, they were already off, but Martin, being a good sort, took the bet anyway. "Number twelve to win, five large," I said, and put the equivalent of three hundred and fifty quid on it to cover my potential loss of two thousand Euros / five thousand quid. It meant that if number twelve came in first, it'd be a winner for the punter. But more importantly, it would be a winner for me too. I'd gone from potentially losing two thousand Euros to potentially winning three thousand.

You guessed it – the horse won. So I went back to Martin to collect my five thousand Euros. I still had to pay the punter his seven thousand, five hundred... but I never saw him again. Whoever he was, he never came to collect his winnings!

I can only assume he backed number twelve, but intended to back number fourteen. He must have been looking at the price of the horse and got confused. He probably watched the race, saw the horse he'd backed lose, and thrown that winning ticket away. I kept expecting to see him the following year, clutching a crumbled ticket in his hand, demanding his money. It does happen sometimes, but he never showed up.

Not for the first time in my working life, I thanked my mother's luck and walked away a richer man. Like they say, at the end of the day, the bookmaker always wins.

AFTERWORD

A bookmaker's life isn't always an easy life, but I count myself lucky to have lived it. Even though I've been successful in my career and in my life, I think I've always been able to stay down-to-earth. What I'm proudest of is not the money that I've made, it's the experiences I've had, and the friends that have come along on my journey with me. I hope you feel like you've got to know a few of the characters I've shared my story with, even if it's just a little bit.

There have been times in my life when I've been sure of my convictions, and I've been firm in putting my foot down. I feel like I had to be resolute to achieve what I was capable of. But my parents set me up to work hard, and I think I've managed that magic mixture of working hard and having a lot of laughs along the way.

I have loved being a bookmaker, and I still love it now, out on the tracks, seeing friends and punters I have known for many years. Colin is always with me, of course. Michelle and David get involved too, and in spite of all the ups and downs in our lives, we've stayed together. David has always been happiest with his head under a bonnet, and he's doing exceptionally well with his own business now. But I'm delighted that Michelle and David often join us at Cartmel – it's the loveliest place in the world when the weather's nice. (And one of the most miserable when it's not.) But we love it there and I sponsor a race at Cartmel every year. Now the next generation of Wadeys are getting involved too. Colin's daughter Lauren has helped us out, and it feels like a proper family affair. Even my dog, Dessie, will be there in 2021, so if you're at Cartmel, come and say hello and bring a treat for the dog!

We love it out there on the racetracks, and I'm certainly glad to have got out of the betting shops when I did. The way of life has changed. Betting shops used to be like social clubs, full of interesting characters and we had a lot of laughs. When the pubs closed at three in the afternoon, they'd come flooding in to place their bets. But they came in for the craic as well. We knew all our customers, we liked most of them. But today's betting shops are more like arcades now. That same sense of companionship has gone.

I feel as if my mother's luck has seen me through some tough times. I've been lucky when so many of the people you've read about haven't. I've lost good friends and acquaintances along the way – far too many of them to cancer – and I hope the contribution we've made to Marie Curie will help some of the people who are touched by cancer today.

Looking to the future, I've invested in three new pitches in 2020. Pitch number four in the Tattersalls ring at Huntingdon, I'll be there on Easter Monday and Boxing Day. An Epsom Derby pitch, number seven in the Tattersalls ring. And county stand, pick six, for the Grand National at Aintree.

I've invested a substantial sum in 2020, even in spite of everything that's happening in the world (and even though I 'retired' from racing back in the early 2000s). Why the big investment? Because, I remain, above all else, the eternal optimist, and I am always looking, with hope, to the future.

Thank you for reading. I hope that all your bets (with other bookmakers) are winning ones, and that you don't lose too much money betting with me!

ACKNOWLEDGEMENTS

I'd like to take this opportunity to offer my thanks and appreciation to: Colin Wakefield, from my cricketing days.

Wally Mills, who taught me how to run a betting shop.

All the managers and staff at my betting shops, including:

Dave Moore

Peter Dagnall (Betting Shop Manager of the Year winner, 1988)

Liam Bennett

Steve Hope

Jean Green

Bonita Bellmon

Debbie Hill

Additional thanks to Chris at Lomas Editorial for his help with this book. **www.lomaseditorial.co.uk**

Just before I go, there's the small matter of that old school photo...

Did you spot me or David Hughes? That's me in the third row back, three in from the left. David is two in from the right in the front row.

MARIE CURIE

As I write this in 2020, dying has become a front-of-mind issue for us all. The Covid-19 pandemic and our ageing population means it's never been more pressing to make sure we have the right care and support in place to be able to protect and cherish each other as we reach the final months, weeks, days and hours of our lives.

The UK's leading end of life charity, Marie Curie is here to support everyone in the UK through all aspects of dying, death and bereavement – and to fight for a society where everyone gets to have the best experience possible at the end of their lives. Marie Curie support the NHS by providing frontline care.

They provide vital bereavement support for family and friends. And they help the nation prepare for death, to help makes things better at the end.

Marie Curie's decades of experience mean they know what it is to die well, and what really matters. Their people have a passion for making sure everyone gets the best possible support – from living with a terminal illness to coping with bereavement.

In 2019, Marie Curie helped more than 60,000 people directly and reached over two million more. Marie Curie/'s:

- Nurses care for people in their homes, giving much-needed respite to overstretched carers.
- Hospices offer the reassurance of specialist care and support in a friendly, welcoming environment – so people can feel safe and cared-for in their final months, weeks and days of life.
- Information and support line help people in their hour of need to feel reassured, informed and empowered to face

what's happening in their lives – whether that's terminal illness, caring or bereavement.

- Campaigns influence decision-makers so people whose lives are touched by terminal illness, death and bereavement have a voice advocating for the change they need to see.

- Research ensures that, as we face what's coming in the years ahead, we understand more about what good end of life looks like, and how we can support each other in the best ways possible – both medically and in the round.

- Public awareness campaigns help change public attitudes to dying, death and bereavement so, as a nation, we can find ways to open the conversation and be better prepared.

IN AID OF

Marie Curie

Care and support
through terminal illness